Y0-BZD-878

Microsoft Office XP/2001/v.X for Teachers

A Tutorial

E. Christine Shinn

Purdue University Calumet

Merrill
Prentice Hall

Upper Saddle River, New Jersey
Columbus, Ohio

Library of Congress Cataloging in Publication Data

Shinn, E. Christine.
    Microsoft Office XP/2001v.X for teachers : a tutorial / E. Christine Shinn.
        p. cm.
    "Word, Excel, PowerPoint for Windows and Macintosh."
    Includes index.
    ISBN 0-13-098743-3
        1. Integrated software. 2. Microsoft Office. I. Title.

QA76.76.I57 S473 2003
005.369—dc21   2002067844

Vice President and Publisher: Jeffery W. Johnston
Executive Editor: Debra A. Stollenwerk
Editorial Assistant: Mary Morrill
Production Editor: JoEllen Gohr
Production Coordination: Carlisle Publishers Services
Design Coordinator: Diane C. Lorenzo
Cover Designer: Robin Chukes
Cover art: Superstock
Production Manager: Pamela Bennett
Director of Marketing: Ann Castel Davis
Marketing Manager: Krista Groshong
Marketing Coordinator: Tyra Cooper

This book was set in Times by Carlisle Communications, Ltd. It was printed and bound by Banta Book Group. The cover was printed by Phoenix Color Corp.

Pearson Education Ltd.
Pearson Education Australia Pty. Limited
Pearson Education Singapore Pte. Ltd.
Pearson Education North Asia Ltd.
Pearson Education Canada, Ltd.
Pearson Educación de Mexico, S.A. de C.V.
Pearson Education—Japan
Pearson Education Malaysia Pte. Ltd.
Pearson Education, *Upper Saddle River, New Jersey*

Copyright © 2003 by Pearson Education, Inc., Upper Saddle River, New Jersey 07458. All rights reserved. Printed in the United States of America. This publication is protected by Copyright and permission should be obtained from the publisher prior to any prohibited reproduction, storage in a retrieval system, or transmission in any form or by any means, electronic, mechanical, photocopying, recording, or likewise. For information regarding permission(s), write to: Rights and Permissions Department.

10 9 8 7 6 5 4 3 2 1
ISBN 0-13-098743-3

About Microsoft Office™ and This Book

Microsoft Office™ (MS Office) is available for both Windows and Macintosh computers. The current Windows version is **Microsoft Office XP™**. If the programs are bought separately, it is equivalent to version 2002—Word 2002, Excel 2002, or PowerPoint 2002. The current Macintosh versions are **Microsoft Office 2001™** for MacOS 9.x or earlier, and **Microsoft Office v.X™** for MacOS X.

This book is designed to provide tutorials to use the MS Office programs in the Windows and Macintosh platforms—MS Office XP, 2001 and v.X. MS Office has different collections of programs between the Windows and Macintosh versions. Also within the Windows versions the included programs are different. The common denominator is Microsoft Word™, Microsoft Excel™, and Microsoft PowerPoint™. Therefore, the tutorials in this book are developed for these programs. More information about MS Office can be found in Chapter 1, "Microsoft Office in Windows and Macintosh."

Features of This Book

This book provides step-by-step tutorial lessons to enhance the hands-on skills of using the common application programs of MS Office and to develop ideas for integrating the programs into teaching and learning. There are six chapters:

- Chapter 1 "Microsoft Office in Windows and Macintosh"
- Chapter 2 "Microsoft Word: The Word Processing Tool"
- Chapter 3 "Graphic Tools and Page Design in Microsoft Office"
- Chapter 4 "Microsoft Excel: The Spreadsheet Tool"
- Chapter 5 "Microsoft PowerPoint: The Presentation Tool"
- Chapter 6 "Database Techniques Using Excel"

All the chapters can be used on both Windows (MS Office XP) and Macintosh (MS Office 2001 and v.X) to achieve the same tasks. MS Office programs—Word, Excel, and PowerPoint—are cross-platform. Therefore, the files can be used between the Windows and Macintosh versions. At the same time, unlike many other application programs, the MS Office programs are not updated simultaneously for the Windows and Macintosh versions. Therefore, they are not completely identical. In cases where minor differences exist, the instruction is specified for the platforms.

A chapter is organized with the following sections:

- **Getting Started.** As an introduction to the chapter, *Getting Started* provides the features of the program, its application in teaching and learning, and the chapter overview.

- **Hands-on Activities.** As the major section of the chapter, the step-by-step hands-on tutorials are to learn how to use the program. There are two to five activities in each chapter.

 When a different instruction is required between the Windows and Macintosh versions, it is indicated by the corresponding icon.

 This icon indicates that there are accompanying files on the CD. For a description of this CD, refer to the next section titled "Supplement: Accompanying CD."

It is always challenging to develop hands-on activities to meet all participants' needs, as their beginning proficiency level varies. Advanced participants may skip some of the hands-on activities. For example, in Chapter 2, "Microsoft Word: The Word Processing Tool," they may skip the first one or two activities. In Chapter 5, "Microsoft PowerPoint: The Presentation Tool," they may skip the first activity if they have created a PowerPoint presentation before.

- **Projects.** At the end of each hands-on activity, there is a project to apply what was covered in the activity. Projects may also be used to test the hands-on activity.

- **Integration with Other Programs.** After the series of hands-on activities and projects, this short section considers how to integrate the program with other programs.

- **Applications.** This section is the summation of the hands-on skills and the ideas of using the program in the classroom with the students and for the teacher's productivity. It can also be used as a brainstorming activity.

- **Summary.** This is a summary of the chapter.

Supplement: Accompanying CD

There is a CD packaged at the back of the book. Throughout the book, when there is a file to refer to on the accompanying CD, it is indicated with the icon. The files are for the hands-on activities, Projects, and Applications.

For the hands-on activities, sample files and QuickTime™ movies are included. The sample files examine the contents in depth or show the finished segments of the instruction. The QuickTime™ movies show the hands-on instruction as an overview in the beginning when the movement on the computer screen is essential (e.g., using drawing tools), and enhance the explanation for the difficult segments in the contents.

For Projects, when it is required to answer the questions or to conduct precise tasks, the answers or the finished sample projects are included in the CD.

For Applications, files are included to support the provided example applications.

Acknowledgments

Many people have contributed their time and knowledge to help in the production of this book. I would like to thank my students, who provided direct and indirect feedback on what works in enhancing their computer technology skills while taking my classes and described how they have applied these skills afterwards.

I deeply appreciate the expert comments and suggestions of the reviewers: Farah Lee Fisher, California State University, Dominquez Hills; John Ouyang, Kennesaw State University; and Chris Peters, Clemson University.

There is a group of people who were willing to do the formative evaluation of this book or to share information with me. I am thankful to Nora Kasprzycki, Deborah Van Slyke, Lisa Olszewski, Maureen Marthaler, Mary Gish, and Gwen Hudson.

My special thanks goes to those who were involved in publishing this book, including Pam Bennett, JoEllen Gohr, Diane Lorenzo, Lisa Hessel, Fawn Weber, and others. I have particularly enjoyed working with the executive editor of this project, Debbie Stollenwerk, who shared insightful thoughts and created a constructive work relationship.

And then, there is my family who gave me unceasing support and encouragement.

Brief Contents

Chapter 1   Microsoft Office in Windows
and Macintosh   1

Chapter 2   Microsoft Word:
The Word Processing Tool   32

Chapter 3   Graphic Tools and Page Design
in Microsoft Office   80

Chapter 4   Microsoft Excel:
The Spreadsheet Tool   129

Chapter 5   Microsoft PowerPoint:
The Presentation Tool   181

Chapter 6   Database Techniques Using Excel   237

Contents

Chapter 1

Microsoft Office in Windows and Macintosh   1

Getting Started   2
Microsoft Office™ and Different Versions   2
Microsoft Office™ and the Platforms   2
What Is New in Microsoft Office XP and 2001?   3
Microsoft Office™ and This Book   4
Overview of This Chapter   4

Activity 1: Navigating Through the MS Office Program   6
Understanding the Platforms and Storage Devices   6
Accessing Programs in MS Office   8
Creating a New Document   9
Keyboard Differences   10
Minimizing/Collapsing the Document Window   11
Restoring the Minimized/Collapsed Document   13
Browsing the Menu and Shortcuts   14
Browsing the Toolbars   15
Understanding the Extension for a File Name   15
Saving a New Document   15
Quitting/Exiting the Program   19
Checking the Saved File (Document)   20
Getting the Disk Out   21
Project 1   22

Activity 2: Desktop Management   23
Opening a File   23
Creating a New Document within the Program   24
Working on Multiple Documents   24
Hiding or Showing the Office Assistant   25
Closing a Document Window   26
Deleting a File   28
Project 2   29

Summary   31

Chapter 2

Microsoft Word: The Word Processing Tool   32

Getting Started   33
Features of Word Processing   33
Word Processing in Teaching and Learning   34
Overview of This Chapter   35

Activity 1: Working with Word Processing   37
Creating a Word Processing Document   37
Selecting the Page Orientation   38
Entering Text   39
Checking Spelling   41
Adding a Header or Footer   42
Viewing the Document in Different Sizes   43
Checking the Print Preview   44
Printing a Document   44
Project 1   44

Activity 2: Editing Text   46
Inserting Text   46
Selecting Text   47
Deleting Text   48
Undoing   48
Moving Text   48
Copying and Pasting Text   49
Saving a Document as You Work   50
Project 2   50

Activity 3: Formatting Text I   51
Viewing the Toolbars   51
Changing Text Alignment   52
Changing Text Appearance   52
Changing Line Spacing   56
Page Break: Adding a Page Break   56
Page Break: Deleting a Page Break   58
Inserting a Page Number   58
Having a Different First Page   59
Adding a Clip Art   60
Changing Margins   62
Saving a Document with a Different Name (Using Save As)   63
Project 3   63

Activity 4: Formatting Text II   65
Indentation: What Is "Indenting a Paragraph"?   65
Indentation: Indenting the First Line with the Tab Key   66
Indentation: Understanding Indentation Markers   66
Indentation: Indenting Whole Paragraphs   67
Indentation: Making a Hanging Indent   68
Table: Adding a Table   69
Table: Changing the Column Size   70
Table: Distributing Columns Evenly   70
Table: Entering Text in the Table   71
Table: Merging Cells   72
Table: Formatting Text in the Table   72
Table: Changing the Row Size   73
Table: Borders and Shading   73
Project 4   75

Integration with Other Programs   76

Applications   77

Summary   79

Chapter 3

Graphic Tools and Page Design in Microsoft Office   80

Getting Started   81
Features of Graphic Programs   81
Graphic Sources and Microsoft Office™   82
Graphic Programs in Teaching and Learning   82
Overview of This Chapter   83

Activity 1: Working with a Drawing   84
Understanding the Drawing Tools in MS Office   84
Drawing Lines   85
Selecting an Object with the Select Objects Tool   86
Deleting an Object   86
Moving an Object   86
Copying and Pasting an Object   87
Drawing Lines with Different Appearances:
    Line Weight, Colors, and Patterns   87
Drawing Squares and Rectangles   88
Filling in an Object with Color and Effects   89
Drawing Objects with the Lines Tool   90
Drawing Objects with the AutoShapes   92
Adding and Editing Text   92
Adding WordArt   93
Creating a 3-D Object   94
Creating a Shadowed Object   95
Formatting an Object: Resizing Manually   95
Formatting an Object: Rotating and Flipping   96
Project 1   96

Activity 2: Grouping Objects in a Drawing   98
Moving Objects to the Front or to the Back   98
Selecting Multiple Objects   99
Grouping Objects   100
Making Changes to the Grouped Object   101
Ungrouping the Object   101
Project 2   101

Activity 3: Formatting a Picture   103
Understanding the Sources of Pictures   103
Getting the Picture Formatting Tools   104
Color Control   105
Filling Color and Effects   105
Brightness and Contrast   106
Picture Effects   107
Cropping a Picture with the Crop Tool   107
Cropping a Picture with Marquees and Lassos   108
Project 3   109

Activity 4: Creating a Page Layout   110
Making Multiple Columns   112
Wrapping Text: WordArt in Line with Text   114
Wrapping Text: Graphic as a Background   115
Wrapping Text: Graphic around the Text   116
Project 4   117

Activity 5: Creating a Web Page   118

Planning a Web Page   118
Preparing the Text   119
Adding Bookmarks   119
Inserting Hyperlinks   120
Completing the Links   122
Previewing the Web Page   123
Saving as a Web Page   123
Project 5   124

Integration with Other Programs   125

Applications   126

Summary   128

Chapter 4	**Microsoft Excel: The Spreadsheet Tool 129**

Getting Started   130

Features of a Spreadsheet   130
Spreadsheets in Teaching and Learning   131
Overview of This Chapter   132

Activity 1: Working with Spreadsheets   133

Creating a Spreadsheet Document   133
Understanding Spreadsheets   134
Entering Data Manually   135
Entering Data with AutoFill Function   135
Using a Mathematical Formula to Calculate Total   136
Using a Function to Calculate Sum (or Total)   136
Understanding Types of Data   140
Creating a Chart   140
Adding a Header or Footer   143
Printing a Spreadsheet   144
Working with the Print Range   145
Project 1   145

Activity 2: Using Spreadsheet Features I   146

Deleting a Chart   146
Using Fill Right   147
Selecting Columns and Rows   149
Sorting Data   149
Changing Text Style   151
Changing Column Width   151
Changing Row Height   152
Formatting the Number (Currency)   153
Formatting Cells: Alignment   154
Adding a Comment to the Cell   155
Project 2   157

Activity 3: Using Spreadsheet Features II   158

Formatting the Number (Date)   159
Inserting or Deleting a Column   159
Inserting or Deleting a Row   161

Calculating the Average   161
Finding the Maximum Value   164
Finding the Minimum Value   166
Formatting the Number (Decimal Precision)   167
Understanding Relative Reference and Absolute Reference   168
Using the Lookup Function   169
Formatting Cells: Merging Cells   172
Formatting Cells: Borders and Shading   174
Project 3   175

Integration with Other Programs   177

Applications   178

Summary   180

Chapter 5

Microsoft PowerPoint: The Presentation Tool   181

Getting Started   182
Features of Presentation Programs   182
Presentation in Teaching and Learning   183
Overview of This Chapter   183

Activity 1: Creating a Presentation with a Template   185
Creating a PowerPoint™ Document with a Template   185
Understanding the Slide Layout   187
Working with Text   188
Viewing the Toolbars   190
Adding Slides   190
Browsing the Slides   192
Viewing the Presentation   192
Project 1   194

Activity 2: Creating a Presentation from Scratch   195
Creating a Blank PowerPoint™ Document   195
Designing the Slide Master   196
Designing the Background   199
Project 2   201

Activity 3: Formatting Presentation I   202
Rearranging the Slides   204
Deleting a Slide   204
Formatting Text: Paragraph Spacing   205
Formatting Text: Indentation   205
Formatting Text: Placeholders   206
Adding Graphics: Clip Arts and Pictures   207
Adding Movies   207
Adding Sounds   208
Adding Animation   209
Adding Custom Animation   211
Adding Slide Transition   218
Project 3   220

Activity 4: Formatting Presentation II   221
Working with an Organization Chart   221
Non-Linear Navigation: Understanding Non-Linear Navigation   224
Non-Linear Navigation: Creating Links with Slide Objects   225
Non-Linear Navigation: Creating Links with Buttons   228
Adding Notes   229
Printing a PowerPoint™ Document   230
Saving as a Web Page   232
Saving as a QuickTime™ Movie   232
Project 4   233

Integration with Other Programs   234

Applications   235

Summary   236

Chapter 6

Database Techniques Using Excel   237

Getting Started   238
Features of a Database   238
Databases, Spreadsheets, and Microsoft Office™   239
Databases in Teaching and Learning   240
Overview of This Chapter   241

Activity 1: Using Spreadsheet as a Database   242
Setting Up a Database   242
Understanding Database Structure   243
Filling in the Form   243
Sorting Data   245
Filtering Data with AutoFilter   245
Filtering Data with Custom Filter   246
Showing All Records   247
Project 1   247

Activity 2: Data Merge   249
Understanding Data Merge   249
Preparing a Word Processing File   249
Preparing a Database File   250
Merging Data: Creating Form Letters   250
Project 2   255

Integration with Other Programs   259

Applications   260

Summary   262

Glossary   263

Index   269

Chapter 1

Microsoft Office in Windows and Macintosh

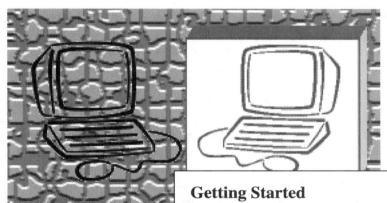

Getting Started
**Activity 1: Navigating Through the
  MS Office Program**
  Project 1
Activity 2: Desktop Management
  Project 2
Summary

Getting Started

 ## Microsoft Office™ and Different Versions

Microsoft Office™ (MS Office) is a collection of software that is initially developed as separate programs but sold as a package. Depending on the package, the included programs are different, but the common and major programs are Microsoft Word™ (Word), Microsoft Excel™ (Excel), and Microsoft PowerPoint™ (PowerPoint).

MS Office is available for both Windows and Macintosh computers. The most current Windows version is Microsoft Office XP™. If the programs are bought separately, it is equivalent to version 2002—Word 2002, Excel 2002, PowerPoint 2002, or Access 2002. This is not to be confused with the new operating system software, Windows XP™. The Windows program runs the computer itself and it is necessary to do any task on the computer, including using the MS Office programs. On the other hand, MS Office programs have particular purposes such as word processing, spreadsheet, or presentation. It is not required to have Windows XP in order to use the Microsoft Office XP. Earlier versions of the Windows program (e.g., Windows ME, 2000, or 98) work.

The most current Macintosh versions of MS Office are Microsoft Office 2001™ and Microsoft Office v.X™. The reason that two versions are coexisting is because of the Macintosh operating system software. Recently Apple Computer™ introduced the new operating system software, MacOS X™ (pronounced "MacOS ten"). Currently a new Macintosh computer is shipped with two versions of the operating system software—MacOS 9.x and MacOS X. The users can choose either version of MacOS. Therefore, it is a transitional period for the Macintosh operating system. While MacOS X promises the more robust system software, not all the existing programs are compatible with this new operating system. Microsoft Office is one example. The MacOS 9.x (and earlier version) users should use MS Office 2001 and the MacOS X users should use MS Office v.X. The two versions of MS Office— 2001 and v.X—are compatible.

 ## Microsoft Office™ and the Platforms

MS Office programs are compatible between the platforms. **Platforms** are types of personal computers such as Windows and Macintosh computers. Word™ in MS Office XP (Windows version) is compatible with MS Office 2001 or v.X (Macintosh version). The same is true for Excel™ and PowerPoint™. In other words, you can create a file on a Windows computer and continue to work on a Macintosh, and vice versa. When the programs are compatible between the platforms, it is referred to as **cross-platform**.

MS Office programs have a unique characteristic in the cross-platform issue. Normally, when a program is cross-platform the same version is used for Windows and Macintosh, (e.g., AppleWorks™ 6.2, DreamWeaver™ 4, HyperStudio™ 4, and so on). When the programs have the same version between the Windows and Macintosh computers, they are identical between two versions. However, MS Office does not seem to have the new version for Windows and Macintosh at the same time, or to use the same version number. Instead, MS Office has a new Windows or Macintosh version in different years with different version names. Therefore, the programs in MS Office are cross-platform, but there are some differences. Fortunately, these differences are minor so that if you know the program in one version, you can use the other version without difficulty.

What Is New in Microsoft Office XP, 2001 and v.X?

In MS Office XP (Windows version), the biggest change is the creation of the **Task Pane**. The Task Pane is shown on the right side of the screen, and it allows a quick access to the functions that are available in the menu. For some tasks the Task Pane is a must, but for other tasks the Task Pane can be hidden. Its contents change depending on the task.

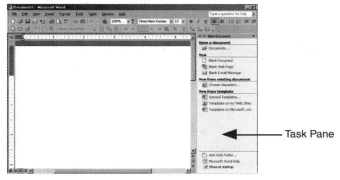

Task Pane

In MS Office 2001 and v.X (Macintosh version), the **Project Gallery** is the starting point in the MS Office programs. When opening a program such as Word™, Excel™, and PowerPoint™, instead of creating a new blank document, it comes to the Project Gallery. From the Project Gallery a new document can be created or a template can be selected. It is like a starting point in an integrated program such as AppleWorks™.

Project Gallery in 2001

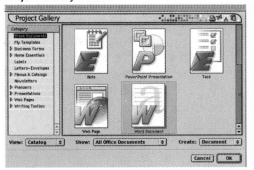

Project Gallery in v.X

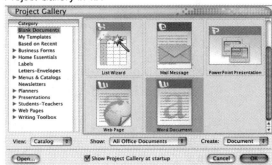

Another change in MS Office 2001 and v.X is the Formatting Palette. The Formatting Palette can be shown or hidden from the View menu. Its contents change depending on the task.

Formatting Palette

In MS Office XP, 2001 and v.X, the Web page creation function has been strengthened. In Word™, automatic typo correction is helpful. As you type, a common mistake can be detected and corrected automatically if AutoCorrect is turned on (Format menu → AutoFormat → AutoCorrect). AutoCorrect is turned on as default, unless you turn it off.

In MS Office XP, the PowerPoint animation has added new features. Using Motion Paths to create animation is new to this version and available only to this version. In MS Office 2001 and v.X, the PowerPoint presentation can be saved as a QuickTime™ movie. This function is available only in the Macintosh versions. However, once the file is saved as a QuickTime™ movie, it can be used on both platforms.

 ## Microsoft Office™ and This Book

This book is designed to provide tutorials for using the MS Office programs and to develop ideas to apply these programs in learning and teaching. The programs selected are those common between MS Office XP (Windows) and MS Office 2001 and v.X (Macintosh): Word™, Excel™, and PowerPoint™. The tutorials are developed to build up experience with the Windows and Macintosh versions by accomplishing the same tasks.

Overview of This Chapter

Although there are only minor differences between the Windows and Macintosh environments, computer users do not feel comfortable going back and forth between Windows and Macintosh. Often they avoid one platform, even though they may be in a situation that requires going back and forth between two platforms. For example, one owns a Windows computer at home and has a Macintosh in the classroom or office. The difference between the Windows and Macintosh is the basic navigation. The navigation means how to get around in the computer environment, such as how to get the disk out of the computer, whether the disk icon appears on the computer screen or not, and a few others. Once computer users understand these minor differences, they will feel much more comfortable using both platforms.

This chapter identifies the navigation differences between Windows and Macintosh through the hands-on activities. Also the navigation differences between MacOS 9 and MacOS X are discussed. It is strongly recommended to review this chapter if you are about to use a platform that you are not familiar with.

Activities, Projects, and Summary

There are two continuing activities. The contents cover the basic computer navigations in the Windows and Macintosh computers. After each activity a project is provided to apply what was covered in the activity. This is followed by the chapter Summary.

Icons to Watch

WIN   **MAC**   When a different instruction is required between the Windows and Macintosh versions, it is indicated by the corresponding icon.

CD   When there is a file on the CD that you can check, it is indicated with the icon.

Activity 1: Navigating Through the MS Office Program

This activity reviews the steps from accessing the program to getting the disk out in the Windows and Macintosh computers. Also, the new features of the MS Office program for the starting point are discussed.

This activity will guide you through the following tasks:

- Understanding the platforms and storage devices
- Accessing programs in MS Office
- Creating a new document
- Keyboard differences
- Minimizing/Collapsing the document window
- Restoring the minimized/collapsed document
- Browsing the menu and shortcuts
- Browsing the toolbars
- Understanding the extension for a file name
- Saving a new document
- Quitting/Exiting the program
- Checking the saved file (document)
- Getting the disk out

CD To browse the tasks that are covered in this activity by viewing a movie, check out the file **Ch1-win** (Windows) or **Ch1-mac** (Macintosh) from the CD. (**Chapter 1** folder → **MoreInfo** folder → **Ch1-win** or **Ch1-mac**)

Understanding the Platforms and Storage Devices

When you finish working on a file, you may want to save it for future use. The file can be saved on the computer hard drive, a floppy disk, a zip disk, a writable CD (CD-R or CD-RW), or the network at school or office. If you use your own computer you can save it on your computer hard drive, but if you are using the computer lab you have to carry the file, or if you want to make a backup copy you may need other storage devices such as floppy disks, zip disks, or CDs. Following is a review of different storage devices—floppy disks, zip disks, and writable CDs.

1. **Floppy disks**. Floppy disks have been available longer than zip disks or writable CDs. However their capacity is limited—1.4 MB (megabytes) for a double-sided, high-density disk. You will need several floppy disks to save the files while going through this book.

   Every disk needs to be formatted to save the information. Some disks are already formatted by the manufacturer. Three types of format are available: unformatted, IBM (or PC) formatted, and Macintosh formatted. Which one then do you need to buy? All three formats work because you can format or reformat the disk for your computer.

   Once the disk is formatted it is either IBM or Macintosh formatted. The IBM formatted disks are for the Windows computers (IBM and IBM compatible computers). When discussing the computer platform, you may find that the terms *Windows computer* and *IBM and IBM compatible computer* are used interchangeably. "Windows computer" is from the software perspective, which is using the Windows operating system. "IBM and IBM compatible computer" is from the hardware perspective. Regardless, the terms indicate the same computer platform, so far. When you work on both Windows and Macintosh platforms, the following information will be helpful in choosing the format of a disk:

		Computer Platform	
		Windows (IBM)	**Macintosh**
Disk Format	IBM	Yes	Yes
	Macintosh	No	Yes

   The Windows computer can read only IBM formatted disks, but Macintosh computers read both IBM and Mac formats. Therefore, if you have to use a Windows computer even for a small amount of work, you have to have an IBM formatted disk.

2. **Zip disks**. Recently, more computers are equipped with a zip drive. The capacity is either 100 MB or 250 MB. 250 MB disks can be used only with a 250 MB zip disk drive, while 100 MB could be used on both 100 and 250 MB zip disk drives. The capacity of a 100 MB zip disk is about the same as 70 floppy disks. For saving the files from this book, one 100 MB zip disk should be enough. In terms of disk format and the computer platform, the same rule applies as the floppy disks.

3. **CD-R** and **CD-RW**. CD-R (Compact Disk-Recordable) and CD-RW (CD-ReWritable) are used to create CD-ROMs. While CD-R can save the information only once and the information is not changeable, CD-RW can be used multiple times. Typically, CDs are good for saving the final product instead of saving data daily. In order to create a CD, a CD-Writer is required. Recently, CD-ROM drive and CD-Writer were combined as one drive. Both CD-R and CD-RW can save up to 700 MB of data.

Accessing Programs in MS Office

There are several ways to access the program in MS Office. Two different methods are discussed here. The first is to open the program by double-clicking the program icon. The second, which is available only for Windows, is to go through Start and launch the program. On Macintosh the first method is the typical way of accessing the program, while the second method is on Windows. Choose one of the following two methods.

Method 1

1. Open the program by double-clicking the icon. Let's open Word:

> **NOTE**   In MS Office v.X you may open a program from the **Dock**. The Dock is a new feature in MacOS X, which is a launching path to open programs, files, and other items that you use often. For example, the Word icon can be placed in the Dock. The following figure is a sample structure of the Dock:

Even when the program icon is not placed in the Dock, when you use the program its icon will appear in the Dock. While a program is being used, the status will be indicated as in the following figure:

> **NOTE**   In MS Office 2001 (MacOS 9 or earlier) if the program does not open by double-clicking the icon, the program is already open. Do the following step:
>
> 1. Pull down the last icon on the right-hand side of the menu bar, and then select Word™:

2. From the **File** menu choose **Quit**.
3. Open Word™ again.

Method 2 (Windows only)

1. Choose **Start** and hold down the mouse.

2. Choose **Programs** (**All Programs**, in Windows XP), and then **Microsoft Word**.

➡ Creating a New Document

Now you are in the program, Word™. Eventually, you will be in the screen to type, but there are middle steps that are different between Windows and Macintosh.

MS Office 2001 and v.X has a new starting point. Instead of creating a blank document, it goes into **Project Gallery**. From Project Gallery, you can choose a document—such as Word™, Excel™, and PowerPoint™—as well as templates. It is like a starting point in an integrated program such as AppleWorks™.

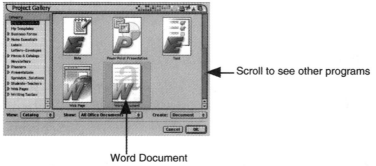

Scroll to see other programs

Word Document

NOTE   In MS Office v.X if you don't see the Project Gallery, it is because the program is already open. Let's quit and start over:
1. From the **Word** menu choose **Quit Word**.
2. Open Word again.

1. Scroll to see other programs.
2. Choose **Word Document**.
   Now you are in a new word processing document.

A new feature in MS Office XP is the **Task Pane**, which is shown in the right side of the screen. Task Pane allows a quick access to the functions that are available in the menu such as creating a new document, opening a document, and others.

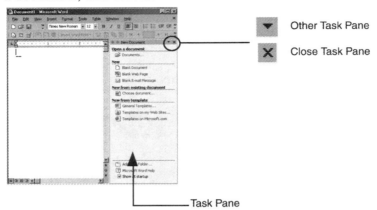

1. Browse other Task Panes. Use the Other Task Panes icon.
2. Close the Task Pane.

   NOTE   To show the Task Pane later, choose Task Pane from the View menu.

3. To get the full size of the screen, click the **Maximize** button.

Maximize button

 Keyboard Differences

There are minor differences in the Windows and Macintosh keyboards. The differences are on the keys Delete/Backspace, Delete/Del, and Return/Enter. Let's compare the differences.

1. Type a few sentences of your choice.

2. Identify the following keys and delete some text.

		Computer Platform	
		Windows (IBM)	Macintosh
Tasks	To delete the text/object from the back of it.	Backspace	Delete
	To delete the text/object from the front of it.	Delete	Del

Backspace key on Windows is the same as **Delete** on Macintosh. They are in the same location on the keyboard. **Delete** key on Windows is the same as **Del** on Macintosh. They are in the same location on the keyboard. Del key on Macintosh is available for the extended keyboard. Some keyboards that come with iMac™ may not have this key.

3. To change the paragraph press **Return** (Macintosh) or **Enter** (Windows). They are in the same location on the keyboard. In this book there will be instructions to press the Return (Macintosh) or Enter (Windows) key. They will be abbreviated as "Press Return/Enter."

Macintosh has both Return and Enter keys. Usually they work the same, but they could have different functions. Windows has two Enter keys.

Minimizing/Collapsing the Document Window

While working on a document, you can visually minimize the document screen. The Windows users refer to this as "**minimizing the window**," while the Macintosh users do not have a defined term, but refer to it as **collapsing the window**. Minimizing/collapsing the document window is useful when you work on multiple documents and want to hide a document temporarily. The minimized/collapsed document window looks different between Windows and Macintosh.

MAC (MS Office 2001)

1. Click the box in the title bar to collapse the window.

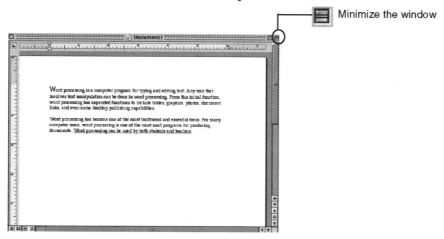

Minimize the window

2. The minimized window will show only the title bar on the computer screen. Unlike Windows, it does not minimize to the status bar in the bottom of the screen.

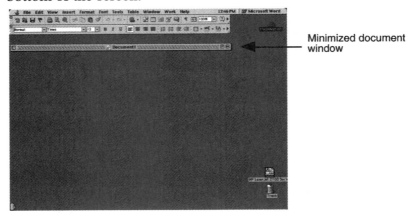

Minimized document window

 (MS Office v.X)

1. Click the button in the title bar to collapse the window.

Minimize the window.

2. The minimized window will appear in the Dock.

Collapsed/Minimized document

1. Click the **Minimize** button.

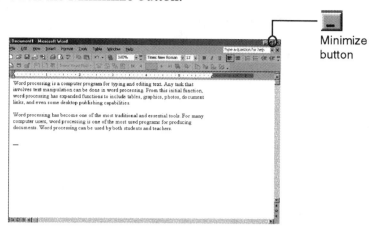

Minimize
button

2. The minimized document name appears in the status bar.

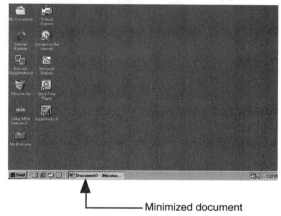

Minimized document

Restoring the Minimized/Collapsed Document

To restore the minimized/collapsed document, do the following steps:

 **(MS Office 2001)**

Click the box in the title bar that you used to minimize the document window.

(MS Office v.X)

Click the minimized/collapsed document in the Dock.

Click the minimized document name in the status bar.

Browsing the Menu and Shortcuts

The menu bar has the collection of functions. On Macintosh you will see the full view of the menu all the time. But on Windows, you may have a half view. To get the full view, hold the mouse and come down to the end of the menu options to choose the arrow mark.

On Windows

To get the full view of the menu.

Using a combination of the keys on the keyboard can perform some of the menu functions. This is called a **shortcut**. On Windows it is the **Control** key plus one or two keys. On Macintosh it is the **Command** ⌘ key (Apple key) plus one or two keys.

Pull down the File menu and browse the shortcuts. Try other menus as well.

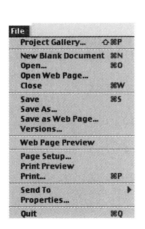

Browsing the Toolbars

Toolbars store commonly used functions. There are many toolbars that have special tasks. Usually these special task toolbars are not shown, but the Standard Toolbar appears on the screen. If you don't see the Standard Toolbar, choose **View** menu → **Toolbars** → **Standard**.

On Macintosh

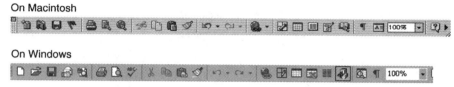

On Windows

 ## Understanding the Extension for a File Name

The Windows computer reads the files only with the appropriate extensions. An **extension** is a three-digit letter to indicate the file type. Therefore, when a document is saved, the proper extension should be added at the end of the file name. For example, the extension for a Word™ file is **.doc**, a PowerPoint™ file is **.ppt**. When a file is saved on a Windows computer, the extension will be remembered automatically—you don't have to type the extension yourself.

On the other hand, the Macintosh computer reads the files with or without the extensions. Therefore, if you use a Macintosh computer, you don't need to add an extension at the end of the file name. However, if you want to work on a Macintosh computer and want to open the file on a Windows computer later, you should add the extension at the end of the file name.

 ## Saving a New Document

The document that you are working on is in the computer memory (RAM: Random Access Memory). It remains in RAM until you quit the program or until the computer is turned off. When the computer is turned off, an unsaved document will be lost. To keep a document for future use, you must save it. A saved document is also referred to as a "file."

Currently, **Document 1** is shown in the title bar. Let's save the document:

1. Choose **Save** (or **Save As**) from the **File** menu.
   Or, choose the Save button from the Toolbar.

2. Identify the following parts of the Save dialog box:

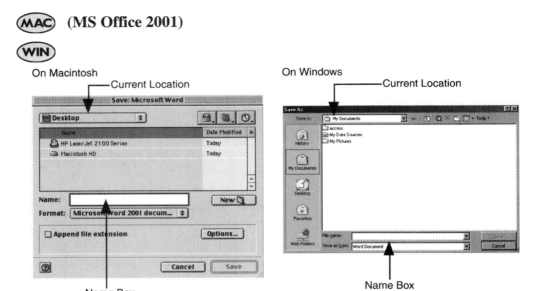

(MAC) **(MS Office 2001)**

(WIN)

- Current Location
  It shows the current location. If you want to see the parent and child folders of that location, click the upside-down triangle. (A parent folder means the place where a file or folder belongs. A child folder is the opposite.) Did you find your current location?
- Name Box
  This is where you type the name of the document.

(MAC) **(MS Office v.X)**

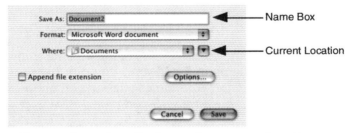

- Current Location: It shows the current location.
- Name Box: This is where you type the name of the document.

3. Let's name Document1 as **FIRST**.
   - Is the File Name Box still highlighted? If so, simply type **FIRST**. It will replace what is in the box.
   - If the File Name Box is not highlighted, delete the word. Then, type **FIRST**.
   - The document name is not case sensitive. Therefore, **FIRST**, **First**, and **first** are considered the same.

   Do not click the **Save** button, yet.

   Do NOT click this button, yet! ➡ **Save**

4. Choose the extension.

   In the Windows environment, an extension at the end of the file name is required. The Windows version application programs add the extension automatically when the file is saved. On Macintosh, files can be read with or without the extension. But if you plan to open the file in the future on a Windows computer, you should add the extension. Also, on Macintosh, the file opens better with the extension if the version of the program is different from the one that the file was created for (e.g., opening a v.X Word file in Word 2001).

   In case you have a file in which you didn't add the extension and you have to open it on Windows, simply add the extension on the file in the Windows computer before opening the file. In MS Office 2001 and v.X (Macintosh versions), you can add the extension by clicking **Append file extension** box in the Save dialog box. As you click the box, the extension will be added at the end of the file name. In this case, the file name will be FIRST.doc.

   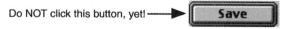
   ☐ **Append file extension**

5. Choose the location to save.

   Do you see the **Save** button in the dialog box? Do NOT click it, yet. Clicking the Save button does not mean that you will save a file in an appropriate place.

   Do NOT click this button, yet! ➡ **Save**

   If you are going to save the document on a disk, make sure the disk is in the disk drive—either a floppy disk or a zip disk.

(MS Office 2001)

5-1. Click the pop-up menu options from the **Current Location**.

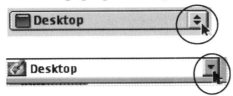

5-2. Choose the location such as Desktop, Hard Drive, Floppy Disk, or ZIP disk.

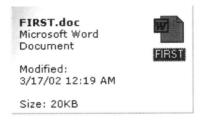

In the above example of the Macintosh computer, the hard drive name is **HARD DRIVE**; the floppy disk name is **My Disk**; and the zip disk is **My ZIP**. Although the Macintosh computer shows the disk names, the Windows computer shows only the generic types of the disks such as 3.5 Floppy (A:), hard drive (C:), or Removable Disk (D:).

 (MS Office v.X)

In the MacOS X environment saving a document on a disk is different from MacOS 9 or Windows. The following steps explain several different locations that you can choose to save a document.

5-1. Choose **Desktop** from the Current Location (Where) options.

5-2. Click the triangle next to the Current Location box to see the full list of the locations.

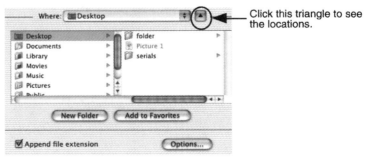

Click this triangle to see the locations.

5-3. Move the bar to the left.

Move this bar to the left.

5-4. Choose the location to save. In the following example, My Zip is selected. The selected location will appear in the Current Location box.

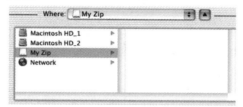

6. Click **Save**.

The dialog box closes and the file name **FIRST** is shown in the title bar.

Quitting/Exiting the Program

When you quit/exit the program, all the files for that program will be closed and you will leave the program. To quit:

 **(MS Office 2001)**

Choose **Quit** from the **File** menu.

 **(MS Office v.X)**

Choose **Quit Word** from the **Word** menu.
(If you are using a different program, the program name will be shown instead of Word. For example, in PowerPoint it is Quit PowerPoint from the PowerPoint menu.)

Choose **Exit** from the **File** menu.

Quit/Exit Word™.

Checking the Saved File (Document)

Are you sure that everything was done correctly and your file FIRST was saved in the right location? Let's check:

1. Open the location in which you saved the file. It could be a floppy disk, zip disk, or hard drive. To open it, double-click the icon.

   The window will appear. Do you see FIRST? If yes, your file FIRST is saved properly.
2. Close the window.

1. Open My Computer (unless you saved the file in My Documents folder). To open it, double-click the icon.

2. Open the location that you saved the file—3.5 Floppy, C, or D drive.

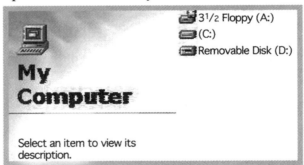

3. Do you see the file FIRST? Click the icon of the file *once* (not twice) to select it.

   It provides the information of the file. Do you see **FIRST.doc** as the file information? The extension was included automatically.
4. Close the window.

Getting the Disk Out

Do this section if you saved the file in a floppy disk or a zip disk.

Now you are ready to get the floppy disk or the zip disk out of the computer. Getting the disks out of the computer is different between Macintosh and Windows. On Windows it is hardware-controlled, while on Macintosh it is software-controlled.

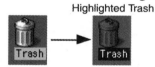 **(MS Office 2001)**

You can choose one of the following two methods:

- **Method 1** (Using **Put Away** Function)
    1. Click the disk—floppy or zip—*once* to select it.
    2. Choose **Put Away** from the **File** menu.

- **Method 2** (Using the **Trash**)
    1. Drag the disk—floppy or zip—icon to the **Trash**, and release the mouse when the **Trash** is highlighted.

Highlighted Trash

Putting the disk into the Trash does not erase the disk. Trash can erase individual files or folders but not the disk itself. Sometimes, this method does not work on a networked computer. Then use Method 1.

NOTE   It is not recommended to use Eject Disk from the Special menu because it can cause some trouble.

 **(MS Office v.X)**

You can choose one of the following two methods:

- Method 1 (Ejecting the disk)
    1. Click the disk—floppy or zip—*once* to select it.
    2. Choose **Eject** from the **File** menu.

- Method 2 (Using the Trash)
    1. Drag the disk—floppy or zip—icon to the **Trash**, and release the mouse when the Trash is changing its icon.

(WIN)

Press the Eject button on the computer next to the disk drive.

Project 1

In this project you will review the basic navigations in the MS Office program. The first part consists of hands-on exercises, and the second part is short-answer questions.

Part 1: Do the following steps.
1. Create a new document with Word™.
2. (Windows only) Close the Task Pane.
3. Type a few sentences of your choice.
4. Minimize/Collapse the window.
5. Restore the minimized/collapsed window.
6. Show the Standard Toolbar.
7. Save the file as **CH1** (add an extension if necessary).
8. Quit/Exit the program.
9. Locate the file CH1.
10. Get the disk out of the computer, if you saved the file on the disk.

Part 2: Answer the following questions.
1. List these storage devices from the largest capacity to the smallest: Floppy disk, zip disk, CD-R.
2. Delete key on Macintosh is the same as _____ key on Windows.
3. Enter key on Windows is the same as _____ key on Macintosh.
4. There are Word™ files titled **WP** and **WP.doc** that were created on Macintosh. Which file can be opened on Windows?
5. On Macintosh, does it make a difference whether you save the file as **WP** or **WP.doc**?
6. On Macintosh, what happens when you put the disk icon into the Trash icon?
7. John bought a zip disk formatted for IBM. Can he use the disk on the Windows or Macintosh computer?
8. John bought a zip disk formatted for Macintosh. Can he use the disk on the Windows or Macintosh computer?

> **CD** To see the answer for Part 2, check out the file **Ch1-Proj1** from the CD. (**Chapter 1** folder → **Projects** folder → **Ch1-Proj1**)

Activity 2: Desktop Management

This activity covers desktop management in and out of the MS Office.

This activity will guide you through the following tasks:

- Opening a file
- Creating a new document within the program
- Working on multiple documents
- Hiding or Showing the Office Assistant
- Closing a document window
- Deleting a file

Before You Begin

Insert the disk that you saved the file FIRST, if necessary.

 ## Opening a File

You can open a file in two ways:

a. Double-clicking the file icon.

b. Opening within the program.
　b-1. Open the program.
　　　For example, if the file is a Word™ file, you have to open Word™ first.
　b-2. Choose **Open** from the **File** menu.
　b-3. Find the file that you want to open.

　　NOTE　When you open a file from a different version of the program from the one that you created the file, use the second method—opening a file within the program. For example, you created a file with MS Office 2001 Word and you want to open it in MS Office XP. Then, you should open Word XP first and then the file (File menu → Open).

Open the file FIRST by using one of the methods described above.

Creating a New Document within the Program

In Activity 1, we discussed how to create a new document. In this section you will create a new document while you are in the program. Currently, you are in Word™. The following instructions show different ways of creating a new document.

Choose one of the following three methods to create a new document:
- Choose **New Blank Document** from the **File** menu.
- Choose **Project Gallery. . .** from the **File** menu. Then, select **Word Document**.
- Use the shortcut in the keyboard. Command ⌘ + N.

Choose one of the following three methods to create a new document:
- Choose **New** from the **File** menu.
- Use the shortcut in the keyboard (Control + N).
- From the Task Pane, choose **Blank Document**.

Create a new document. Do not close the document that you are currently using.

 Working on Multiple Documents

When you work on more than one file, either from the same program or different programs, it is not necessary to close a file in order to open another. This is the same for Windows and Macintosh.

Let's explore how to go back and forth among documents.

1. Let's use the **Window** menu.
   Pull down the Window menu. It will show the document names that you are currently working on. In this example, Document 1 and FIRST.doc are the document names. Choose the document name that you want to see.

2. Besides the Window menu, you can also directly click inside the document.
   If you don't see the other document because of the one on top, you can move the top document. To move the document, click the title bar where you see the document name on top of the document window, hold down the mouse, and drag it.

3. (MS Office 2001 and XP only) If you are working with multiple programs, you can choose the **Application** menu to select the program as well. Application menu is located at the end of the right-hand side of the menu bar.

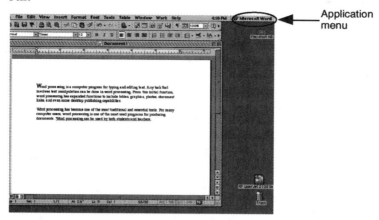

Application menu

You will see the programs. At least you will see Word™ that you are currently using. In this example, Word™ and PowerPoint™ are running.

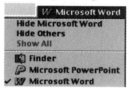

4. (MS Office v.X only) If you are working with multiple programs, you can select the program from the Dock.

5. You can also open the minimized/collapsed documents.

 Hiding or Showing the Office Assistant

In the MS Office programs, the **Office Assistant** gives feedback for the questions that you type in the box or makes suggestions while you work. It can also be hidden. The following steps show how to hide and show the Office Assistant temporarily:

MAC

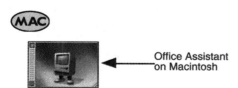

Office Assistant on Macintosh

- In MS Office 2001, to turn off/on the Office Assistant, choose **Turn Assistant Off/On** from the **Help** menu.
- In MS Office v.X, to turn off/on the Office Assistant, select or unselect **Use the Office Assistant** from the **Help** menu.

You can also hide the Office Assistant by clicking the Close Box. Then, when the Office Assistant has to say something, it will come back.

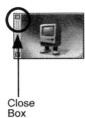

Close
Box

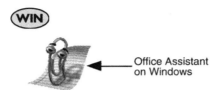

Office Assistant
on Windows

To hide the Office Assistant:
1. Choose **Hide the Office Assistant** from the **Help** menu.
2. If you get the following message about turning off the Office Assistant, click **No, just hide me**.

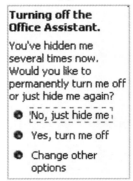

Turning off the Office Assistant.

You've hidden me several times now. Would you like to permanently turn me off or just hide me again?

● No, just hide me

● Yes, turn me off

● Change other options

To show the Office Assistant:
• Choose **Show the Office Assistant** from the **Help** menu.

 ## Closing a Document Window

Closing a document window means to close the document, not to minimize it. The document window can be closed by choosing **Close** from the **File** menu or by clicking the **close box**. The close boxes on Windows and Macintosh are located in the opposite direction.

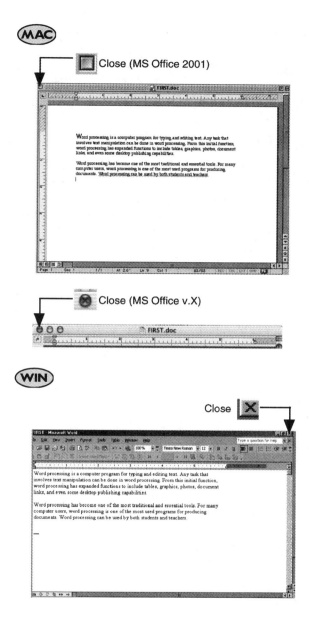

When you have more than one document for the same application, closing the window will simply close the file and the other files will still be open.

Let's close a document window—Close DOCUMENT1.
(Do not save the file when the computer is asking.)

Now there is only one document left, FIRST. When you close the last document, it will be different between Windows and Macintosh. On Windows what will happen depends on which Close box you will choose—**Close** or **Close Window**. If you choose Close, only the document will be closed and the program—in this case, Word™—will still be running. On the other hand, if you choose Close Window, it will close the document and quit the program. Therefore, it is the same as quitting the program.

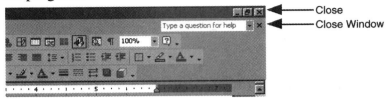

On Macintosh there is only one kind of Close box. It works like Close Window on Windows. Therefore, it simply closes the document, but the program is still running. On Macintosh the program runs until you choose to quit the program.

Let's Quit/Exit the program Word™.

 ## Deleting a File

You can delete a file. The place to put the file is **Recycle Bin** (Windows) or **Trash** (Macintosh). Both icons are on the computer Desktop.

On Windows   On Macintosh

Let's delete the file FIRST.

1. Select the file FIRST by clicking it *once.*
   (If you click twice, the file will be opened.)

2. Drag the file FIRST icon into Trash and release the mouse when the Trash is highlighted.

   Highlighted Trash

   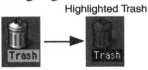

   If you release the mouse when the Trash is not highlighted, the file does not go into the Trash. Instead, it may be placed on the Desktop or another location on the computer.

3. Putting the file in the Trash does not erase the file. The file stays there until you empty the Trash. Let's empty the Trash:
   3-1. Choose **Empty Trash** from the **Special** menu (MacOS 9 or earlier) or the **Finder** menu (MacOS X).
   3-2. Click **OK** to the confirmation message.

1. Select the file FIRST by clicking it *once*.
   (If you click twice, the file will be opened.)

2. Choose one of the following two methods:
   - Drag the file FIRST into Recycle Bin and release the mouse when the Trash is highlighted.

   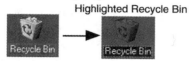

   If you release the mouse when the Recycle Bin is not highlighted, the file does not go into the Recycle Bin. Instead, it may be placed on the Desktop or another location on the computer.
   - Choose **Delete** from the **File** menu.

3. Click **YES** to the confirmation message.

4. Putting the file in the Recycle Bin does not erase the file. The file stays there until you empty the Recycle Bin. Let's empty the Recycle Bin:
   4-1. Open the Recycle Bin.
   4-2. Choose **Empty Recycle Bin** from the **File** menu.
   4-3. Click **YES** to the confirmation message.
   4-4. Close the Recycle Bin.

Finishing Touches

Get the disk out of the computer, if you used the disk.

Project 2

This is a continuing project from Project 1. The first part consists of hands-on exercises, and the second part is short-answer questions.

Part 1: Do the following steps.
1. Open the file CH1.
2. Create a new Word™ document while you are in CH1. (Do not quit/exit or close CH1.)
3. Go back and forth between the new document—Document—and the file CH1.
4. Hide the Office Assistant.
5. Close the newly created document window.
6. Quit/Exit the program.
7. Delete the file CH1.
8. Erase the file CH1 from the Trash or Recycle Bin.

Part 2: Answer the following questions.

1. You have two files currently open and are working on one of them. What happens in the following scenarios?
    1-1. On Macintosh, you click the **Close** box of the file that you are working on.
    1-2. On Windows, you click the **Close** box of the file that you are working on.
    1-3. On Windows, you click the **Close Window** box of the file that you are working on.

2. You have only one file currently open. What happens in the following scenarios?
    2-1. On Macintosh, you click the **Close** box of the file that you are working on.
    2-2. On Windows, you click the **Close** box of the file that you are working on.
    2-3. On Windows, you click the **Close Window** box of the file that you are working on.

To see the answer for Part 2, check out the file **Ch1-Proj2** from the CD. (**Chapter 1** folder → **Projects** folder → **Ch1-Proj2**)

Summary

1. In MS Office programs—Word™, Excel™, and PowerPoint™—there are few differences between Windows and Macintosh versions. Because these programs are cross-platform, it is possible to create a file on one version and continue to work on the other.

2. There are some differences in navigation between Windows and Macintosh computers, as well as between MacOS 9 and MacOS X.

3. From the hands-on activities, the following tasks were covered:
   - Creating a new document
   - Keyboard differences between Windows and Macintosh
   - Understanding the platforms and storage devices
   - Browsing the menus, shortcuts, and toolbars
   - Document Windows
     - Closing a document window
     - Minimizing/Collapsing the document window
     - Restoring the minimized/collapsed document
     - Working on multiple documents
   - Saving a document
     - Saving a new document
     - Understanding the extension for a file name
     - Checking the saved file (document)
   - Quitting/Exiting the program
   - Getting the disk out
   - File management
     - Opening a file
     - Deleting a file
   - Hiding or Showing the Office Assistant

Microsoft Word: The Word Processing Tool

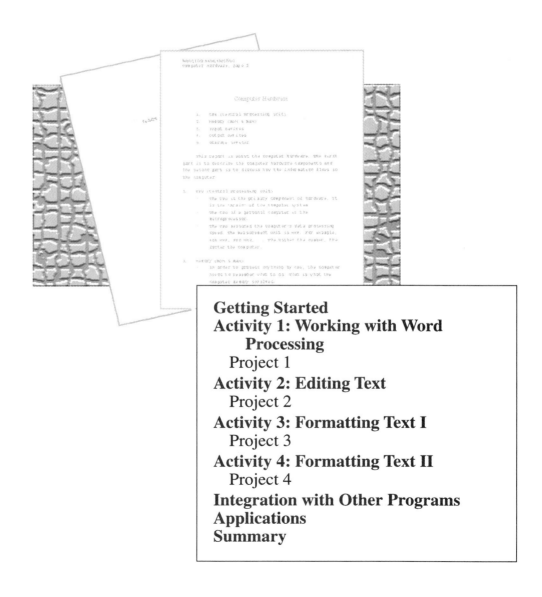

Getting Started
**Activity 1: Working with Word
     Processing**
   Project 1
Activity 2: Editing Text
   Project 2
Activity 3: Formatting Text I
   Project 3
Activity 4: Formatting Text II
   Project 4
Integration with Other Programs
Applications
Summary

Getting Started

 Features of Word Processing

Word processing is a computer program for typing and editing text. For many computer users, word processing is one of the most used programs for producing documents. Any task that involves text manipulation can be done in word processing. From this initial function, word processing has expanded features to include tables, graphics, photos, document links, desktop publishing capabilities, and web page development.

The features of word processing programs can be summarized as follows:

- **Basic word processing functions**
  - Typing text and saving it for future use
  - Word wrap: It allows continuous typing without watching the end of a line so that the word will go down to the next line if there is not enough space.
  - Checking spelling and using the thesaurus

- **Modifying text**
  - Deleting and inserting text
  - Searching and replacing word(s)
  - Copying and moving text: Instead of retyping text, you can move the text to another location or you can copy the text to have the identical text in another location.

- **Formatting text**
  - Text appearance: Text size, font, style (bold, italic, underline, etc.), and color can be selected.
  - Justification (alignment): The text can be aligned to the left margin (this is the default), to the center, to the right margin, or to both the left and right margins.
  - Indentation: Adjust the beginning of the paragraph to start with the full length or to leave space.
  - Header, footer, and page numbering: Header or footer contains the repeating information such as the title of the document and the automatic page number.

- **Page layout**
  - Inserting graphics
  - Inserting tables
  - Multiple columns: Normally, a word processing file has a single column. It can be formatted for multiple columns.
  - Wrapping text around the graphic: This is to design the appearance of text and graphic as a page layout.

- **Saving as a web page**
  This is a modern feature in word processing programs. A word processing document can be saved as a web page. What you see in the word processing document will be translated into a web page.

A word processing program is available as a stand-alone program (e.g., Microsoft Word™, Corel WordPerfect™) or as part of integrated software, such as Apple-Works™ or MicrosoftWorks™. All word processing programs have similar basic capabilities. Therefore, after learning word processing with one word processing program, it is easy to adapt to other word processing programs.

 ## Word Processing in Teaching and Learning

Word processing is used in classrooms at all levels of education across the subject areas. The primary applications of word processing are to deal with text. A few examples of how students can use word processing are as follows:

- Keyboarding
  Keyboarding is using the fingers properly for typing. When students learn keyboarding skills, a word processing program is used. Important issues related to keyboarding (and word processing) are when to introduce it to students and how to balance it with the development of handwriting.

- Writing tool
  - Students can learn how to write a research paper, including the title page, appropriate headings/subheadings, references, header, and page numbers.
  - Students can write a story.
  - Students can write a book report.
  - Students can write a letter.
  - Students can create a résumé.

- Editing and revision
  - Students can edit and revise papers based on the teacher's feedback.

- Keeping text for future use
  - Students can keep articles for their classroom newspaper.
  - Students can keep text information for their web pages.

- Collaborative group activities
  - Students can brainstorm the ideas by typing in thoughts, moving the text (thoughts) to sort, and deleting the unselected thoughts.
  - Students can work on a group project for writing, researching, and reporting.

Teachers can use word processing for instructional activities with the students' participation as indicated in the preceding examples. Also, teachers can use word processing for instructional material development and for classroom management:

- Teaching language and writing skills
  - Teachers can give a word processing file with two to three paragraphs and ask the students to revise the paragraphs to make the writing more coherent and effective.
  - Teachers can teach letter-writing technique, including different parts of a letter and how to prepare an envelope.
  - Teachers can teach how to write a research paper in an appropriate format, including a citation style for references and bibliography.

- Preparing the course materials
  - Teachers can create lesson plans, handouts, test questions, presentation materials, and syllabi.

- Administrative use
  - Teachers can write a report, a memo to parents, and other written documents.

- Developing templates for instructional and administrative use
  - Teachers can develop templates to collect information in a uniformed style. It is like using a printed form, but it allows the teacher to collect information in the computer file instead of writing it on the paper.

 ## Overview of This Chapter

Activities and Projects

There are four continuing activities. The sequence of the activities begins with simple word processing tasks and moves to text formatting features. After each activity a project is provided to apply what was covered in the activity.

Applications, Integration with Other Programs, and Summary

At the end of the chapter, the Applications section can be used for brainstorming and developing ideas to use word processing in teaching and learning. This is followed by the Integration with Other Programs and Summary sections.

Icons to Watch

(WIN) **(MAC)** There are only a few differences between the Windows and Macintosh versions of Word™. When a different instruction is required, it is indicated by the corresponding icons.

(CD) When there is a file on the CD that you can check, it is indicated with the icon.

More Information

Word™ has access to graphic features—drawing and picture editing. Learning how to use the graphic tools and creating the page layout in word processing will be discussed in Chapter 3 "Graphic Tools and Page Design in Microsoft Office."

Activity 1: Working with Word Processing

This activity is a lesson on the basic features of word processing and how to apply the functions that we discussed in Chapter 1 "Microsoft Office in Windows and Macintosh" to create a report with word processing that is based on the following scenario:

> "A group of students—Group 1—are working on a report about the functions of the computer hardware components."

This activity will guide you through the following tasks:

- Creating a word processing document
- Selecting the page orientation
- Entering text
- Checking spelling
- Adding a header or footer
- Viewing the document in different sizes
- Checking the print preview
- Printing a document

If you are familiar with the contents covered in this activity, you may skip the activity, but you may want to complete Project 1 at the end of the activity.

 Creating a Word Processing Document

(The following is a short instruction for creating a word processing document. If you need a detailed instruction, see Chapter 1 "Microsoft Office in Windows and Macintosh" → Activity 1 → *Creating a New Document* section.)

    1. Open **Word**™.

Microsoft Word

2. Open **Word Document** from the Project Gallery.

1. Open **Word**™.

Winword

➔ Selecting the Page Orientation

Page orientation is choosing the direction of the page, either vertical (also referred to as *portrait*) or horizontal (*landscape*). The default is the vertical orientation. Because we usually use the vertical orientation, we don't have to select the direction for each word processing document. However, if you should choose the horizontal direction, it is better to set up before you work on the document.

Vertical (Portrait)

Horizontal (Landscape)

To select the page orientation:

1. Choose **Page Setup. . .** from the **File** menu.

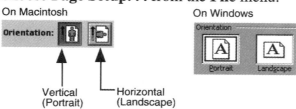

2. For this activity, we will stay with the vertical direction. Click **OK** to close the dialog box.

 Entering Text

1. Understanding the Text Insertion Point.

   In a word processing document, the blinking **text insertion point** indicates where you are going to enter text. The text insertion point is a form of the cursor. The cursor can be shown in different shapes.

   | text insertion point

2. Before typing in text, let's review a few things.
   - The ending of a line may be different on your screen, and that is OK. Do not press the Return/Enter key, except when you change the paragraph.
   - Leave *one* space after a period. It used to be two spaces after a period, but one space has become more common.
   - Use uppercase and lowercase. To type uppercase (capital letters), hold down the Shift key from the keyboard and type the letter.
   - To erase misspelled characters:

     Use **delete** or **del** key from the keyboard.

     Use **Backspace** or **Delete** key from the keyboard.
     To review the differences of these keys, see Chapter 1 "Microsoft Office in Windows and Macintosh" → Activity 1 → *Keyboard Differences* section.
   - To make a bullet (•):
     1. Choose **Symbol. . .** from the **Insert** menu.

        Choose Symbols Tab

        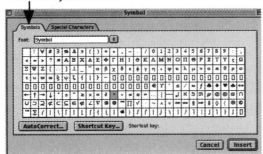

     2. Choose the bullet (•).
     3. Click **Insert**.
     4. Click **Close**.
        NOTE   The shortcut for making a bullet is Alt+0149 (Windows) or Option+8 (Macintosh).

- Word™ has an automatic formatting function to enter bullets and numbers sequentially in each paragraph. This function is either loved or hated. Although the function is useful, it can be in your way when you don't want the sequential numbers or bullets. Let's turn off this function for this activity:
  1. Choose **AutoFormat. . .** from the **Format** menu.
  2. Click **Options**.

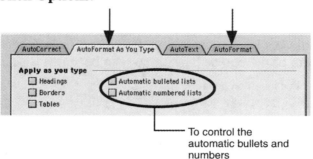

To control the
automatic bullets and
numbers

  3. From the **AutoFormat As You Type** tab, unselect **Automatic bulleted list** and/or **Automatic numbered list**.
  4. From the **AutoFormat** tab, unselect **Automatic bulleted list**.
  5. Click **OK**.

     NOTE   To turn on the automatic bulleted or numbered function, simply select the options from the same tabs.

3. Type the following paragraphs. (After a number or a bullet, to get the space, press the **Tab** key once, instead of pressing the space bar several times.)

```
This report is about the computer hardware. The first
part is to describe the computer hardware components
and the second part is to discuss how the information
flows in the computer.

1.   CPU (Central Processing Unit)
•    The CPU is the primary component of hardware. It is
the "Brain" of the computer system.
•    The CPU of a personal computer is the
microprocessor.
•    The CPU measures the computer's data processing
speed. The measurement unit is MHz. For example, 400
MHz, 500 MHz, . . . . The higher the number, the faster
the computer.

2.   Memory (ROM & RAM)
•    In order to process anything by CPU, the computer
needs to remember what to do. That is what the computer
memory involves.
•    There are two kinds of computer memory: ROM (Read
Only Memory) and RAM (Random Access Memory).
```

```
3.  Input Devices
•   Input devices are used to enter data into the
computer. Examples of input devices are keyboard,
mouse, joystick, graphic pad, touch screen, scanner,
and voice recognizer.

4.  Output Devices
•   Output devices are used to see the results of
entered data. Examples of output devices are monitors
and printers.

5.  Storage Devices
•   Storage devices are used to keep the work for
future use. Examples of storage devices are hard disks,
floppy disks, ZIP disks, and writable CDs.
```

> **CD** To learn more about how the auto-formatted number or bulleted lists
> work, check out the files **AutoFormat1** and **AutoFormat2** from the CD.
> (**Chapter 2** folder → **MoreInfo** folder → **AutoFormat1** / **AutoFormat2**)

Checking Spelling

A dictionary in the word processing program is used to check the spelling in the document by comparing typing with the words in the dictionary and finding unknown words. In Word™ it is possible to check the grammar along with the spelling.

Let's check spelling:

1. Choose **Spelling and Grammar. . .** from the **Tools** menu.

2. If there is no questionable word, the following message will appear.

On Macintosh

On Windows

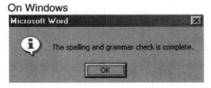

If there are questionable words, the dialog will appear:

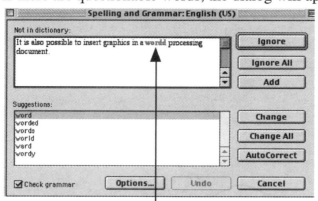

Questionable word

If there is no questionable word, simply click **OK** in the dialog box. If there is a questionable word, the word will be highlighted in the dialog box.

3. What to do with the questionable word?

Apply the following options to your document:

- If the word is correct, click `Ignore` (Macintosh) / `Ignore Once` (Windows).
- If you want to ignore the same questionable word in the document, click `Ignore All`.
- If the word is incorrect and the right word is shown in the suggestions, choose the word by clicking it. Then, click `Change`. The word will be replaced.
- If the word is incorrect and no suggestion is right, simply type the correct word over the questionable word. Then, click `Change`.

Adding a Header or Footer

A **header** is an element of the page that appears on top of the printed page. Various information can be included: text, graphic, automatic page number, and current date and time.

The same information can be placed in the bottom of the page. That is called a **footer**. A header or a footer will be shown in every page of the document.

Let's add **your name**, **class name**, and **class time** in the header:

1. Choose **Header and Footer** from the **View** menu.
   A separate area for the header will appear along with the tools. The header is separated from the main text.

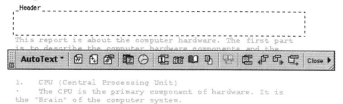

2. Type **your name**, **class name**, and **class time** in the header.

3. Click **Close** to go back to the main document.
   Header appears in a lighter color. But when you print, it will print the color that you used (if you use a color printer).

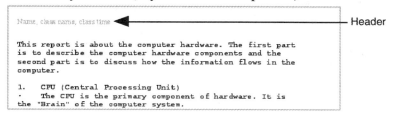

Header

NOTE To choose the footer, click the button (Switch between Header and Footer).

Header or Footer

Viewing the Document in Different Sizes

You can view the document in different sizes. It can be adjusted from the Standard Toolbar. Normal size is 100%. The higher the number, the bigger the size. Try different viewing sizes.

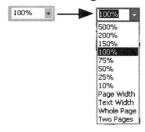

→ Checking the Print Preview

Before printing the document you can check the layout of the page by using the **print preview** option. Let's check the page view of your document:

1. Choose **Print Preview** from the **File** menu.
2. Click **Close** to close the print preview option.

→ Printing a Document

Make sure that your computer is connected to a printer.

1. Choose **Print. . .** from the **File** menu.
2. Click **Print** (Macintosh) or **OK** (Windows).

NOTE   The shortcut for printing is Control+P (Windows) or +P (Macintosh).

Finishing Touches

1. Save the file with the name **WORD1**.
   (If you need instruction, see Chapter 1 "Microsoft Office in Windows and Macintosh" → Activity 1 → *Saving a New Document* section.)

2. Quit/Exit the program.
   (If you need instruction, see Chapter 1 "Microsoft Office in Windows and Macintosh" → Activity 1 → *Quitting/Exiting the Program* section.)

3. Check whether **WORD1** is saved properly.
   (If you need instruction, see Chapter 1 "Microsoft Office in Windows and Macintosh" → Activity 1 → *Checking the Saved File* section.)

Project 1

In this project you will create a word processing document and enter the information about the Food Guide Pyramid.

1. Create a new Word™ document.
2. When you type text in word processing, you should remember the following:
   • Do NOT press the Return/Enter key at the end of a line.
   • Leave one space after a period.
   • Use upper- and lowercases.
   • Turn off AutoFormat for bulleted lists and numbered lists.

3. Choose the Landscape (horizontal) page orientation.
4. Type the following paragraph.

```
The Food Guide Pyramid is built from five food groups.
These five food groups are:
1.   Bread, cereal, rice & pasta group,
2.   Vegetable group,
3.   Fruit group,
4.   Milk, yogurt, & cheese group, and
5.   Meat, poultry, fish, dry beans, eggs, & nuts group.

Then there is the fats, oils, & sweets group, which is
not part of the five food groups but appears in the
Food Guide Pyramid.
```

5. Check spelling.
6. Add footer.
   Type your name and other information (e.g., class time).
7. Check the document layout.
   (File menu → Print Preview)
8. Save the document as **WP1**.
9. Print the document.

> CD To see a finished sample project, check out the file **WP-Proj1**
> from the CD. (**Chapter 2** folder → **Projects** folder →
> **WP-Proj1**)

Activity 2: Editing Text

Activity 2 will continue to use the file that was created in the previous activity, WORD1, to explore text editing features.

File needed for this activity: WORD1

This activity will guide you through the following tasks:

- Inserting text
- Selecting text
- Deleting text
- Undoing
- Moving text
- Copying and pasting text
- Saving a document as you work

If you are familiar with the contents covered in this activity, you may skip the activity, but you may want to complete Project 2 at the end of the activity.

Before You Begin

1. Open the file **WORD1**.
   (If you need instruction, see Chapter 1 "Microsoft Office in Windows and Macintosh" → Activity 2 → *Opening a File* section.)

   If you skipped Activity 1, you can copy the file WORD1-1 from the CD to your disk, and then open it. (**Chapter 2** folder → **MoreInfo** folder → **WORD1-1**)

2. Turn off the automatic bulleted and numbered format.
   (Use AutoFormat. . . from the Format menu.)

Inserting Text

You can insert text anywhere in a word processing document. To insert text in the document, bring the text insertion point to the place where you want to insert text. You may move the text insertion point by

a. Moving the mouse and clicking the mouse at the right place, or
b. Pressing the arrow keys on the keyboard.

Let's add the title `Computer Hardware` at the beginning of the page, and leave an extra line between the title and the rest of the text as in the following figure:

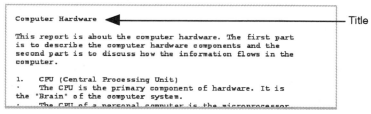

1. Bring the cursor (the text insertion point) to the top of the text, in front of the paragraph. `"This report is about the computer hardware."`
2. Type the title **Computer Hardware**.
3. Press the Return/Enter key twice in order to leave a blank line.

Add the following text at the end of the document as in the following figure:

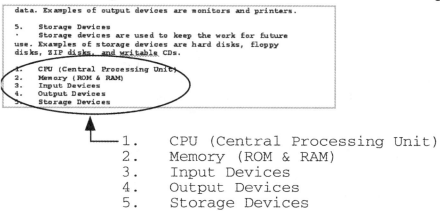

```
1.    CPU (Central Processing Unit)
2.    Memory (ROM & RAM)
3.    Input Devices
4.    Output Devices
5.    Storage Devices
```

➡ Selecting Text

To make changes in the text—to delete, copy, or change the appearance of the text, the text should be selected first. To select text, bring the cursor in front of the text that you want to select and drag the mouse across the text, and then release the mouse. The text will be selected (highlighted). You may select a character, words, phrases, sentences, and even the whole text in the document.

Besides dragging the mouse, you can also click the mouse to select text. If you click a word twice, the whole word will be selected. If you click anywhere in a paragraph three times, the whole paragraph will be selected.

Select the first two paragraphs as in the following figure:

Deleting Text

Deleting text is removing the text permanently from the document. You may delete a character, words, phrases, sentences, and even the whole text in the document.

You learned how to delete characters by pressing the Delete (Macintosh) and Backspace keys (Windows) from the keyboard, as well as Del (Macintosh) and Delete (Windows) keys. There is an easy way to delete more than one character at a time. To delete text, first identify the text that you want to delete. That is selecting the text and then deleting the selected text.

Let's delete the text:

1. Are the paragraphs still selected from the previous step?
2. Press the **Delete** key (Macintosh) or **Backspace** key (Windows). Were the paragraphs deleted?

 ## Undoing

If you made a mistake, choose **Undo** from the **Edit** menu after the unwanted action. It comes with various undo functions such as undo typing, undo formatting, or others, depending on what you have just done. This will recover your mistake. You can keep selecting Undo to recover more than one mistake.

You have just deleted the paragraphs. Let's undo deleting:

1. Choose **Undo Typing** from the **Edit** menu.
   Were the paragraphs recovered?

Moving Text

Text can be moved from one location to another location within the document or to another document. There are two methods for moving text:

a. Cut and Paste
b. Drag and Drop

Cut and Paste is moving the text by using the commands from the menu. **Drag and Drop** is literally dragging the text and dropping it in a new location.

1. Let's move the text in the bottom of the page to underneath the title by using **Cut and Paste** method. When you finish, it should look as follows:

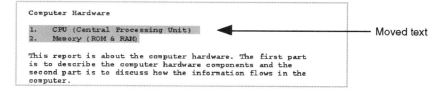

1-1. Select the text in the bottom of the page.

```
1.    CPU (Central Processing Unit)
2.    Memory (ROM & RAM)
```

1-2. Choose **Cut** from the **Edit** menu.

1-3. Set the cursor in the next line of the Title. (Click the blank line underneath the Title.) Press Return to leave a blank line.

1-4. Choose **Paste** from the **Edit** menu.

2. Let's move the text in the bottom of the page to underneath the title by using **Drag and Drop** method. When you finish, it should look as follows:

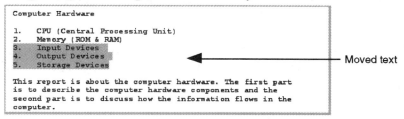

Moved text

2-1. Select the text in the bottom of the page.

```
3.    Input Devices
4.    Output Devices
5.    Storage Devices
```

2-2. Click inside the selected text and hold down the mouse.

2-3. Drag the selected text to the new location.

2-4. Release the mouse.

> **CD** To learn more about how moving text works when the auto-formatting function is used, check out the file **AutoFormat3** from the CD. (**Chapter 2** folder → **MoreInfo** folder → **AutoFormat3**)

 ## Copying and Pasting Text

You can have the same text in different locations in the document without typing it again. A word, a sentence, a paragraph, or even the whole text can be copied and pasted. First, the text to be copied should be selected. Second, the commands **Copy** and **Paste** from the **Edit** menu should be used.

Let's copy the title `Computer Hardware` and paste in the header. When you finish, it should look as in the following figure:

```
Header
Name, class name, class time
Computer Hardware
```

1. Select the title `Computer Hardware`.

2. Choose **Copy** from the **Edit** menu.

3. Choose **Header and Footer** from the **View** menu.

4. Set the text insertion point after Class time in the header.
5. Press the Return/Enter key to go down to the next line.
6. Choose **Paste** from the **Edit** menu.
7. Close the header.

 Saving a Document as You Work

Why do you need to save the document (file) again? In Activity 1, you saved the file as WORD1. Then you made changes on WORD1 in this activity. The computer memory (RAM) remembers these changes. But, it is not on your file WORD1, yet.

You should define the file name only when saving the file for the first time. After that you don't have to give the file name again, unless you want to save it as a different name. Saving the changed information is simpler than saving the information the first time.

It is a good idea to save the changes often—every 5 to 10 minutes—when you work on a long document. It prevents the loss of the work in case of power failure or other accidents.

Let's save the changes on WORD1:

1. Choose **Save** from the **File** menu.
   You do not see any dialogue box. The computer saves the changes automatically under the file name WORD1. Your file WORD1 has been updated.

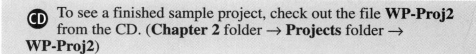
Project 2

In this project you will continue to work on the Food Guide Pyramid to apply more word processing features.

1. Open the file **WP1**.
2. Insert the title Food Guide Pyramid before the paragraph that you typed.
3. Add an extra line between the title and the rest of the text.
4. Copy and paste the title Food Guide Pyramid to the footer, next to your name.
5. Save the file.

> To see a finished sample project, check out the file **WP-Proj2** from the CD. (**Chapter 2** folder → **Projects** folder → **WP-Proj2**)

Activity 3: Formatting Text I

Activity 3 will continue to use the file that was created in the previous activity, WORD1, to explore text formatting features.

File needed for this activity: WORD1 (after Activity 2)

This activity will guide you through the following tasks:

- Viewing the toolbars
- Changing text alignment
- Changing text appearance
- Changing line spacing
- Page break: Adding a page beak
- Page break: Deleting a page beak
- Inserting page number
- Having a different first page
- Adding a clip art
- Changing margins
- Saving a document with a different name (Using Save As)

Before You Begin

Open the file WORD1.

If you skipped Activity 2, you can copy the file WORD1-2 from the CD to your disk, and then open it. (**Chapter 2** folder → **MoreInfo** folder → **WORD1-2**)

 ## Viewing the Toolbars

Let's show the toolbars that you need to use for this activity—Standard Toolbar and Formatting Toolbar. From the **View** menu, choose **Toolbars** → **Standard** (or **Formatting**).

On Windows, if the toolbars are not shown in two rows, choose the option at the end of the toolbar, and select **Show Buttons on Two Rows**.

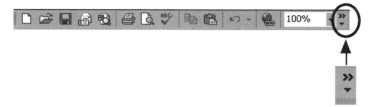

Changing Text Alignment

Text alignment is how to line up the text—to the left, to the right, to both sides, or to the center. The text alignment can be changed by using the alignment options from the Toolbar.

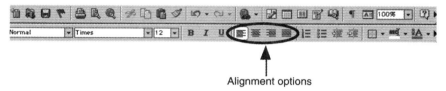

Alignment options

Identify the following icons from the toolbar as the alignment options:

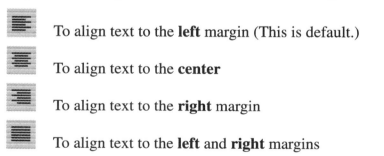

To align text to the **left** margin (This is default.)

To align text to the **center**

To align text to the **right** margin

To align text to the **left** and **right** margins

Let's center the title `Computer Hardware:`

1. Select the title `Computer Hardware`.
2. Click the **center alignment** icon from the ruler.

Changing Text Appearance

Text appearance can be determined by font, size, style, color, and shade.

1. **Font**. The **Font** can be chosen from the Toolbar. On Macintosh you can use the Font menu as well.

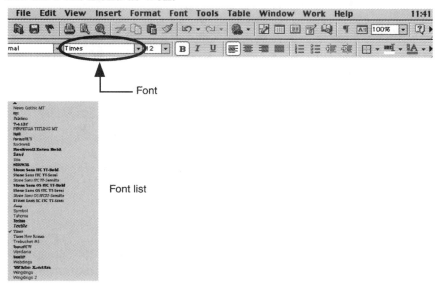

The font list shows the names of the fonts along with their looks. It is also called WYSIWYG (What You See Is What You Get). The font that you are currently using is checkmarked (√). Also, the font name is shown in the box.

2. **Size**. The font size can be changed from the Toolbar. The font size is measured by **points**. The larger the number of points, the larger the size of the text. The default is 12 points.

3. **Style**. You can apply one or more styles in the text. The style options include Plain Text, **Bold**, *Italic*, <u>Underline</u>, ~~Strikethrough~~, Outline, Shadow, Superscript, and Subscript. The default style is Plain Text. You may combine several styles. For example, you can choose bold and italic for the same text. The styles used most often—Bold, Italic, Underline—are located in the Toolbar.

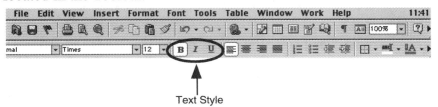

More style options are in the **Format** menu → **Font** → **Font** tab.

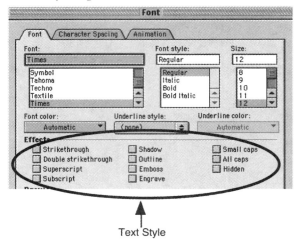

Text Style

Plain Text is the default style. If you want to cancel the style that was used, you may choose the style again. For example, if you want to cancel the underline, select the underlined text and then choose Underline again.

4. **Color**. Default text color is black. Of course, you can choose different colors. To see the text printed in color, you need a color printer. With a black-and-white printer, the text will be shown as a gray tone.

Text color

5. **Highlight**. You can add a highlight in the text. Default is No-shade.

On Macintosh   On Windows

Let's change the style of the title `Computer Hardware` to Times New Roman 18 points, bold, and color. See the following instructions. When you finish, it should look as in the following figure:

Formatted title

1. To change the title `Computer Hardware` to Times New Roman 18 points:
   1-1. Select the title `Computer Hardware`.
   1-2. From the Toolbar, choose **Times New Roman** for the font.
   1-3. (While the title is still selected) From the Toolbar, choose **18 point**.

2. To change the title `Computer Hardware` to the bold style (while the title is still selected) choose Bold from the Toolbar.

3. To change the text color of the title (while the title is still selected) choose a different color from the Toolbar.

Let's add highlight (shade) to the subtitles. See the following instructions. When you finish, it should look as in the following figure:

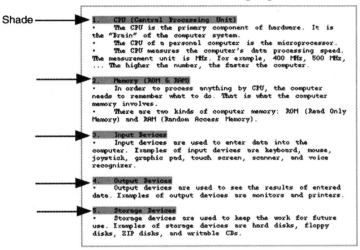

1. To highlight the first subtitle:
   1-1. Select the first subtitle, `1. CPU (Central Processing Unit)`.
   1-2. Choose the Highlight button from the Toolbar. Choose a light color, such as light gray.

2. Apply the shade for the rest of the subtitles.

Changing Line Spacing

Line spacing is the space between the lines. The single-spaced line is default. You can increase this space with the Line-Spacing options in the **Format** menu → **Paragraph. . .** → **Indents and Spacing** tab.

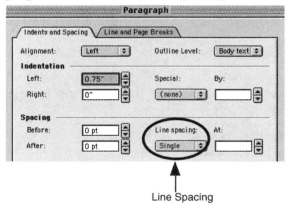

Line Spacing

Let's increase the space between lines to 1.5 lines:

1. Select the whole text, except the header. (Header is separated from the main text.)
2. Choose **Paragraph. . .** from the **Format** menu.
3. Choose the **Indents and Spacing** tab.
4. Select 1.5 lines from the Line-Spacing options.

5. Click **OK**.
   The text is now in two pages:

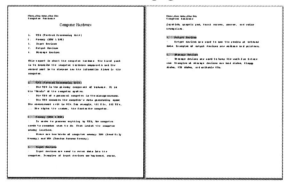

 ## Page Break: Adding a Page Break

A **page break** is a mechanism to divide pages manually. When a page is full, the computer moves to the next page automatically. But if you would like to type text in the next page before the current page is full, you can add a page break manually.

Let's add a title page for the Computer Hardware report, and then add a page break between the title page and the main report.

1. Set the cursor (text insertion point) before the title `Computer Hardware`.

2. Press the Return/Enter key about 5 times to leave some space.

3. Type text for the title with the centered alignment as follows:

```
Report: Computer Hardware
         Group 1
        Maria Casa
        Silvy Post
         Tate Lee
```

The page should look as in the following figure:

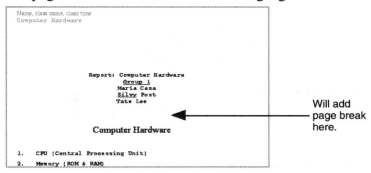

Will add page break here.

4. Place the cursor where you want to add a page break (see the preceding figure).

5. From the **Insert** menu, choose **Break → Page Break**.

Click **OK**.

Now you have a separate page for the title. Scroll up and down to see the pages. There are three pages:

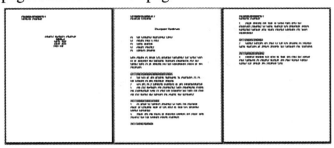

6. Add one more page.

An extra page is placed between the title page and the main report. There will be four pages:

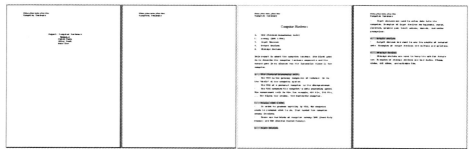

→ Page Break: Deleting a Page Break

As you can add a page break, you can also delete a page break.

Let's delete page 2—the extra blank page between the title page and the main report. That means you have to delete the page break between pages 2 and 3, or pages 1 and 2. Let's delete the page break between pages 2 and 3:

1. Bring the text insertion point to the beginning of the main text (not in the header) in page 3—the main report page.

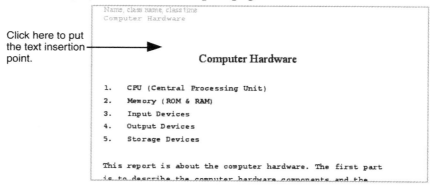

2. Press the **Delete** key (Macintosh) or **Backspace** key (Windows).

→ Inserting a Page Number

Inserting page number is to let the computer calculate the page number of the document and place the page number in each page. The page number can be placed in the header or the footer.

Let's insert page number after the word page in the header.

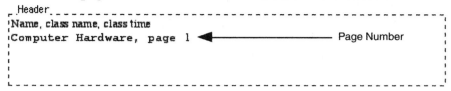

1. Choose **Header and Footer** from the **View** menu.

2. After Computer Hardware, type: **, page.**

3. Add one space after **page.**

4. Click **Insert Page Number** button.

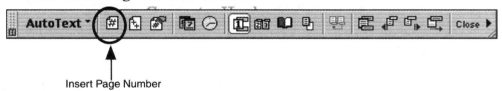

Insert Page Number

5. Click **Close.**

6. Check the page number in each page.

> **NOTE** Normally, the page number begins from 1. However, if you need to begin the page with a different number you can define it.
>
> 1. Choose **Page Numbers. . .** from the **Insert** menu.
>
> 2. Click **Format...** .
> 3. Type in the appropriate page number in the dialog box:
>
>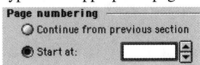
>
> 4. Click **OK.**

 ## Having a Different First Page

Scroll up and down and see the header in the pages. All the pages have the same header. Sometimes a header is not needed in the title page—first page.

Let's have a different look in the first page:

1. Access the Different first page option.

   From the **Format** menu, choose **Document** → **Layout** tab.

From the **File** menu, choose **Page Setup** → **Layout** tab.

2. Check **Different first page**.

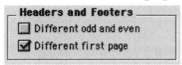

3. Click **OK**.

Scroll up and down the pages. Do you see the difference in the title page—first page? The first page does not show the header. But it still counts the page number. Therefore, page 2 shows the page number 2.

Adding a Clip Art

A **clip art** is a graphic that is ready to be used. MS Office™ has a collection of clip art that you can use. Also, you can copy and paste other clips from different sources. If you do so, be aware of the copyright. Some clip arts are free to use, but many others are not.

Let's add a clip art to the title page. See the following instructions. When you finish, it should be similar to the following figure:

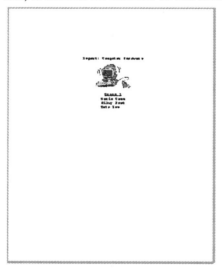

1. Place the cursor (text insertion point) where you want to add a clip art.

2. From the **Insert** menu, choose **Picture → Clip Art. . . .**
   Clip Gallery dialog box appears.

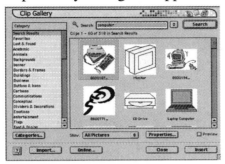

3. Search a clip art of your choice by using:
   a. List in the left side of the dialog box
   b. Search box to type in the possible title of the clip art

4. When you find the right clip art, click the clip art.

5. Click **Insert**.
   The clip art will be inserted in your document.

1. From the **Insert** menu, choose **Picture → Clip Art. . . .**

2. Search a clip art of your choice by using:
   a. Search box
   b. Clip Organizer

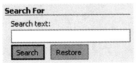 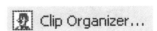

To search the clip art by titles, use the Search box:
   1. Type in a title of the clip arts. The matching clip arts will be shown
      in the Task Pane.

   2. When you find a clip art to use, simply click the clip art, then it will
      be placed in the document.

If you want to see the clip art collection, use the Clip Organizer. To use the Clip Organizer:

1. Click **Clip Organizer**.
2. Choose **Office Collections**.

3. Click the **Collection List** to see the clip arts.

4. When you find a clip art to use, drag and drop the clip art to the document.

Changing Margins

A **margin** is the empty space between the edge of the paper and the information on the paper.

Let's check the current margins and change them:

1. Access the margin control.

   From the **Format** menu, choose **Document** → **Margins** tab.

   From the **File** menu, choose **Page Setup** → **Margins** tab.

2. The current margins are shown:

   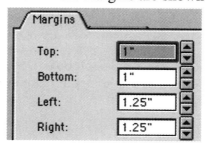

   Current margins are 1 inch for the top and bottom; 1.25 inches for left and right.

3. Let's change Top margin to 1.5 inches.
   3-1. Type **1.5** in the appropriate margin box.
   3-2. Click **OK**.

Compared with a 1-inch margin, a 1.5-inch margin has more empty space between the edge of the paper and the text. This indicates that the space for the text is smaller per page with a bigger margin. Go through the pages. You may notice that there is more space between the header and the main text after you increase the margin.

Saving a Document with a Different Name (Using Save As)

There are two different commands for saving a document—**Save** and **Save As** from the File menu. What are the differences between **Save** and **Save As**?

When saving a document the first time, **Save** and **Save As** are the same.

However, after the file is saved, it is different.

- If you choose **Save**, new changes will be saved under the current file name automatically. Therefore, the information in the current file will be updated. The new version will replace the old one. You have done this before in Word Processing Activity 2. You saved the work of Activity 2 under WORD1. In fact, you are still using WORD1 file.

- If you choose **Save As** after the file name is given, you can give a different file name or save the file in a different location. Then, the old file will remain as it is, and the new file will save the current information. This is useful when you want to modify the file but do not want to lose the original. For example, when you teach a class you can start the lesson plan from the previous semester's lesson plan file. You may add or delete the information. At the same time you don't want to lose the previous semester's lesson plan. Then, you can use Save As to create another file for the current lesson plan.

Let's save your work with a different file name:

1. Choose **Save As** from the **File** menu.
2. Name the document as **WORD3** (because this is Activity 3 and there is no file named WORD2).
3. Select the right location—such as your disk—to save the document.
4. Click **Save**.

Project 3

This is a continuing project of Word Processing Project 2 to format the text.

1. Open the file **WP1**.
2. Save the file as **WP3**.
3. Change the page orientation to Portrait (vertical).

4. Add a page that will serve as the title page.
   - It should be the first page.
   - Have the title `Food Guide Pyramid`.
   - Choose the Center alignment for the title.
   - Have your name.
   - Highlight your name.
   - Choose your own choices of font, size, and color for the title and your name.
   - Add a clip art.
5. Insert a page break at the end of the title page so that the title page does not have other text that you entered before. There will be two pages—Title and the second page.
6. In page 2, make the title `Food Guide Pyramid` center aligned, Arial 18 point, Bold and Shadow in style. You can choose a different color, if you want to.
7. Enter the following text after the existing text in the document with **1.5** line spacing. Before typing the text, add a blank line between the existing text and the new text. Make sure to insert the bullets. Use the Tab key to leave space after a bullet.

   `Recommended Servings`

   `The Food Guide Pyramid also shows the recommended`
   `servings for each food group per day:`
   - `Bread, cereal, rice & pasta group: 6-11 servings`
   - `Vegetable group: 3-5 servings`
   - `Fruit group: 2-4 servings`
   - `Milk, yogurt, & cheese group: 2-3 servings`
   - `Meat, poultry, fish, dry beans, eggs, & nuts group: 2-3 servings`
   - `Fats, oils, & sweets group: Use sparingly`

8. Make the following changes to the footer:
   - 8-1. Add the page number in the footer next to `Food Guide Pyramid`. Make sure to have one space before the page number.
   - 8-2. Change the appearance of the footer: Helvetica 10 point, Plain text.
9. Make the first page look different—do not show the footer.
10. Change the top and bottom margins to 1.25 inches.
11. Save the file.

> ⓒⒹ To see a finished sample project, check out the file **WP-Proj3** from the CD. (**Chapter 2** folder → **Projects** folder → **WP-Proj3**)

Activity 4: Formatting Text II

This is a continuation from Activity 3. The major contents of formatting in this activity are making indentations and working with a table.

File needed for this activity: WORD3

This activity will guide you through the following tasks:

- Indentation: What is "Indenting a Paragraph"?
- Indentation: Indenting the first line with Tab key
- Indentation: Understanding Indentation Markers
- Indentation: Indenting whole paragraphs
- Indentation: Making a hanging indent
- Table: Adding a table
- Table: Changing the column size
- Table: Distributing columns evenly
- Table: Entering text in the table
- Table: Merging cells
- Table: Formatting text in the table
- Table: Changing the row size
- Table: Borders and shading

Before You Begin

1. Open the file WORD3.

2. Save the file as WORD4.
   Save the file often during the activity.

 ## Indentation: What Is "Indenting a Paragraph"?

Indentation means leaving spaces in the beginning of a line or a paragraph.

- You can indent the first line of a paragraph by pressing the Tab key. This function is useful when you make an indentation for the first line of the paragraph only.
- You can also indent the whole paragraph, including the first line. Or you can indent the whole paragraph but not the first line.

Indentation: Indenting the First Line with the Tab Key

Let's indent the paragraph below the numbered list, as in the following figure:

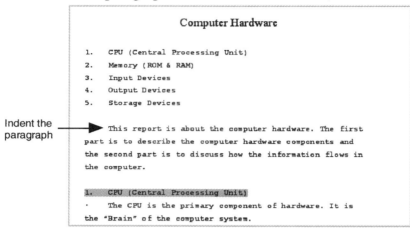

1. Set the cursor (the text insertion point) in the beginning of the paragraph.
2. Press the **Tab** key.

 ## Indentation: Understanding Indentation Markers

The **Indentation Markers** allow (1) indentation of the whole paragraph or (2) indentation from the second line of the paragraph. The indentation markers are located below the title bar.

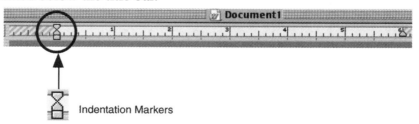

Indentation Markers

The indentation markers have three parts—top triangle, bottom triangle, and the rectangle below the bottom triangle. The top triangle controls the first line of the paragraph. The bottom triangle controls the rest of the lines in the paragraph. The rectangle controls the whole paragraph. When you move the rectangle, both triangles will move.

Let's review the functions of the Indentation Markers. Do not apply it on your document, yet. Compare the location of the Indentation Markers.

1. Indenting the first line of a paragraph.
   This is the same as using the Tab key as you did in the previous section. It is often easier to use the Tab. The location of the indentation markers and the formatted text (highlighted text) are as follows:

2. Indenting the whole paragraph.
   You can indent the whole paragraph.

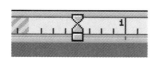

3. Hanging Indent.
   You can indent the whole paragraph, except the first line. This is called a **hanging indent**.

To learn more about the indentation by viewing a movie, check out the file **Indentation** from the CD. (**Chapter 2** folder → **MoreInfo** folder → **Indentation**)

 Indentation: Indenting Whole Paragraphs

Let's indent the paragraphs under the title for 0.5 inch as in the following figure. See the instructions that follow.

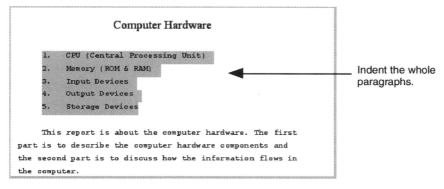

Indent the whole paragraphs.

1. Select the text as highlighted in the preceding figure.

2. Drag the bottom part of the indentation markers (the one looks like a rectangle) to 0.5 inches in the ruler. This rectangle part moves both the upper and lower triangles at the same time.

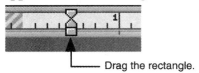

Drag the rectangle.

You can also move the top triangle first, then the bottom one.
Were all the paragraphs indented?

 ## Indentation: Making a Hanging Indent

Let's make a hanging indent for the text under the title of 1. `CPU` (`Central Processing Unit`) as in the following figure.

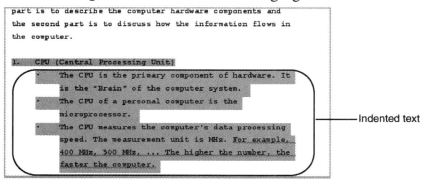

Indented text

The first line is 0.5 inch indented, and the rest of the paragraph is 1.0 inch indented. This is to begin the first line along with the title (not the number of the title) and to indent the rest of paragraph for 0.5 inch.

1. Select the text to indent. See the preceding figure.
2. Move the upper triangle to 0.5 inch and the lower triangle to 1.0 inch.

Repeat the same hanging indent for all the paragraphs for each subtitle. When you finish, it should be as in the following figure. You may have different endings for some lines, but the general layout of the text should be the same.

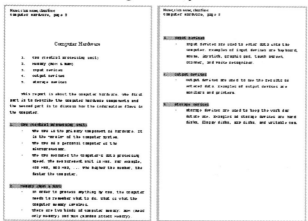

 ## Table: Adding a Table

A **table** is composed of blocks in which you can enter and arrange the data, such as text or graphic. The following figure is an example of a 3 Rows × 3 Columns table. **Rows** run horizontally and **columns** vertically. Each block is called a **cell**. In the following table, there are nine (9) cells.

Let's add a table at the end of 2 . Memory (ROM & RAM) section to compare ROM and RAM.

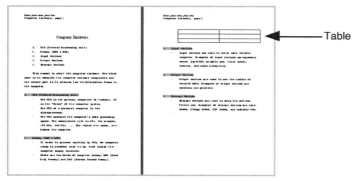

— Table

1. Click where you want to add a table.
   Press the Return/Enter key, if you need to make a space before the table.

2. From the **Table** menu, choose **Insert → Table. . . .**
   Insert Table dialog box appears.

3. Define the size of the table.
   In this example, there will be two columns and three rows.

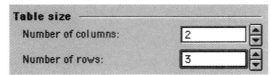

4. Click **OK**.
   A table is entered. (For this activity, if the table is between two pages insert a page break before the table.)

Table: Changing the Column Size

Let's indent the table for 1 inch by changing the size of the first column.

1. Click the border of Column 1.
   The cursor changes as in the following figure:

To change the column size

2. Hold the mouse and drag it 1 inch.
   As you drag the mouse, so does the ruler. Therefore, it would be easier to use other indented text as a guideline for 1 inch. In this activity, you can align the table with the indented text, not the bullets.

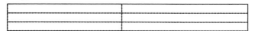

The table is indented and one column is bigger than the other.

 NOTE   In this section and the previous one—adding a table and changing the column width—a table was created and indented. Macintosh users can simplify these two steps into one by placing the indentation markers in the right place before adding a table.

Table: Distributing Columns Evenly

Currently, one column is bigger than the other. Let's make both columns the same size.

1. Select the table.
2. From the **Table** menu, choose **AutoFit → Distribute Columns Evenly**.

Table: Entering Text in the Table

Let's enter data in the table:

1. Type in text for the following cells.

Memory	
ROM	RAM

- Don't worry about formatting for now.
- To move to the next cell, either click the cell or press the Tab key. (In Word™, within the table the Tab key does not leave a defined space. Instead, it moves to the next cell.)

2. Let's prepare text for cell 5.
   When finished, the table will look as in the following figure. See the instructions that follow.

Memory	
ROM	RAM
• Permanent memory (information cannot be added or deleted) • Not very important to know the capacity when we buy the computer	

The text has bullets and space with the Tab key. But we cannot use the Tab for spacing inside the table. Therefore, let's type the text outside the table and move it into the table.

2-1. Type the following text outside the table. Use Tab between the bullet and the text. The ending of each line may be different.

- Permanent memory (information cannot be added or deleted)
- Not very important to know the capacity when we buy the computer

2-2. Select the typed text.
2-3. Move the selected text to the cell. (Use Drag and Drop, or Cut and Paste)

3. Prepare text for the last cell.
   When finished, the table looks as in the following figure. See the text to be typed below the figure.

Memory	
ROM	RAM
• Permanent memory (information cannot be added or deleted) • Not very important to know the capacity when we buy the computer	• Temporary memory (available while the computer is on) • Very important to know the capacity when we buy the computer

```
       •    Temporary memory (available while the computer is
    on)
       •    Very important to know the capacity when we buy
    the computer
```

➡ Table: Merging Cells

Merging cells is to combine two or more cells into one.

Let's combine the cells in the first row. The finished table should be as follows:

Memory		◄── Merged cell
ROM	RAM	
• Permanent memory (information cannot be	• Temporary memory (available while the	

1. Select the cells to be merged.
   Click the first cell, and then drag the mouse to the next cell.

Memory		◄── Select the cells
ROM	RAM	
• Permanent memory (information cannot be	• Temporary memory (available while the	

2. Choose **Merge Cells** from the **Table** menu.

➡ Table: Formatting Text in the Table

Let's format the text in the table as follows. See the instructions below.

Memory	
ROM	RAM
• Permanent memory (information cannot be added or deleted) • Not very important to know the capacity when we buy the computer	• Temporary memory (available while the computer is on) • Very important to know the capacity when we buy the computer

1. Align the text in Row 1 with centered alignment.
   1-1. Select Row 1.
   1-2. Choose the **Centered** alignment.

2. Align the text in Row 2 with centered alignment.

3. Format Row 3 with a hanging indent of 0.25 inch.

Table: Changing the Row Size

The row size can be changed in the same way as the column size. Make Row 2 bigger as in the following figure:

Memory	
ROM	RAM
· Permanent memory (information cannot be added or deleted) · Not very important to know the capacity when we buy the computer	· Temporary memory (available while the computer is on) · Very important to know the capacity when we buy the computer

◄———— Bigger Row Size

 ## Table: Borders and Shading

Borders are the lines around the cells. **Shading** is filling in color in the cell. Both borders and shading are used often to format a table.

In this activity Rows 1 and 2 will be formatted with the border and shading as in the following figure. See the instructions that follow.

Memory	
ROM	RAM
· Permanent memory (information cannot be added or deleted) · Not very important to know the capacity when we buy the computer	· Temporary memory (available while the computer is on) · Very important to know the capacity when we buy the computer

Let's add shading in Row 1.

1. From the **View** menu choose **Toolbars → Tables and Borders**.

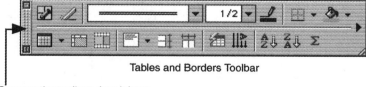

Tables and Borders Toolbar

To move the toolbar, drag it here.

2. Select Row 1.

3. Choose Shading Color from the toolbar.

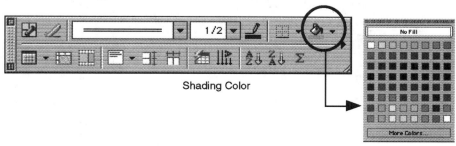

Shading Color

Let's add a 0.5-point double line as a border in the bottom of Row 2.

1. Make sure to keep the Tables and Borders Toolbar on the screen.

2. Select Row 2.

3. Select a double line from the **Line Style** in the toolbar.

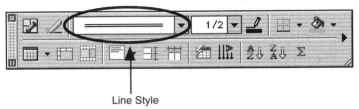

Line Style

4. Choose ½ pt from the **Line Weight**.

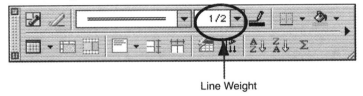

Line Weight

5. In the toolbar, select the **Borders → Bottom Border**.

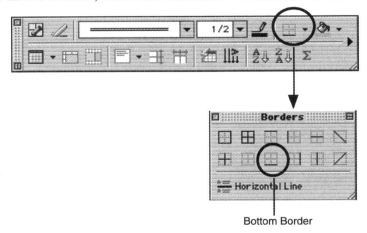

Bottom Border

When finished, close the Tables and Borders Toolbar.

Finishing Touches

Save the document.

Project 4

This is a continuation from Word Processing Project 3 to apply more formatting options.

1. Open the file **WP3**.
2. Save the file as **WP4**.
3. In page 2, under the `Recommended Servings` heading, indent the bulleted text for 0.5 inch with the Indentation Markers.
4. Add a page break at the end of the text to add a new page.
5. In the new page, add the following sentence.

> `The examples of food items in each group are summarized`
> `in the following table:`

5-1. Indent the first line of the paragraph with the Tab key.
6. Add a table after the newly added paragraph.
   * Indent the table for 0.5 inch.
   * Enter the text and format it as in the following table.
   * Format the table—row size, bordering, and shading.

Food Guide Pyramid	
Food Group	**Food Items**
• Bread, cereal, rice & pasta group	Bread, muffin, pizza crust, crackers, pretzels
• Vegetable group	Lettuce, broccoli, cabbage, spinach, carrots
• Fruit group	Apple, peach, pear, grape, orange, watermelon
• Milk, yogurt, & cheese group	Ice cream, yogurt, cottage cheese
• Meat, poultry, fish, dry beans, eggs, & nuts group	Beef, chicken, pork, salmon, peanuts
• Fats, oils, & sweets group	Butter, sugar, jam, soft drink, candy

7. Save the file.

> **CD** To see a finished sample project, check out the file **WP-Proj4** from the CD. (**Chapter 2** folder → **Projects** folder → **WP-Proj4**)

Integration with Other Programs

Integration of word processing with other application programs can be achieved in many ways. The most frequent method is to insert elements from other application programs into a word processing document. The main purpose of such integration is to support the text information in the word processing document.

One example is to insert a graphic into a word processing document. The graphic can be clip art, images developed with other graphic programs, scanned pictures, and digital photos from a digital camera. Recently, word processing programs have access to graphic tools as a part of integrated software (e.g., AppleWorks™) or as shared tools in a bundled software package (e.g., Microsoft Office™).

The text saved in word processing can also be integrated into other programs such as web authoring, page layout, or presentation. For example, when you create web pages, it is easy to compose text information in word processing and then copy and paste the text into a web-authoring program. Although a word processing file can be saved as a web page, it is more common to use web-authoring programs for creating professional web pages.

The data and chart generated in spreadsheet can also be copied and pasted in word processing as well. Often this is to support the text description with the numeric data from spreadsheet.

Also, when a word processing file is used with a database file, data merge can be performed to generate form letters or labels. This will be discussed in Chapter 6 "Database Techniques Using Excel."

Applications

In this chapter, word processing hands-on skills and the ideas of using word processing in the classroom were discussed. Examine the possibilities of applying word processing in education.

1. Collect ideas on how to use word processing with the students. You can refer to the section *Getting Started* to create your own ideas. Consider the following example to get started:

Example

Activity Purpose: To correct the grammar in English or in foreign language (e.g., French, Spanish, German, . . .) classes.

Activity Description: The teacher prepares a word processing file that has sentences or short paragraphs and gives the file to the students. The students will correct the grammar in the file. To distinguish the original from the revision, the students use different text styles or colors. For example, the students can cross out the original words by using the strikethrough style (~~strikethrough~~) and type the new words in plain text with a different color.

(Note: In Word™ the strikethrough style can be accessed from the Format menu → Font.)

2. Collect ideas on how to use word processing as a teacher for classroom management and teaching. You can refer to the section *Getting Started* to create your own ideas. Consider the following example to get started:

Example

Activity Purpose: To develop templates.

Activity Description: Teachers can develop templates for lesson plan or period schedule. To see examples, check out the files **Lesson** and **Schedule** from the CD.

(**Chapter 2** folder → **Applications** folder → **Lesson** and **Schedule**)

3. Create a lesson plan in which you can integrate word processing by expanding the ideas in the section *Getting Started* or by developing your own ideas. Include the following components:
   - Subject matter
   - Grade level
   - Purpose of the activity (lesson objective)

- Target audience
  - Prior knowledge on the lesson objective (any related content covered?)
  - Computer skill
  - Any other information that you want to include
- Environment
  - Location: In the classroom or in the lab?
  - Number of computers needed
- Description of instructional activity
  - Description on how the lesson will proceed and how word processing will be used

4. Collect ideas on how to integrate word processing with other programs. You can refer to the section *Integration with Other Programs* to create your own ideas.

Summary

1. Word processing is a computer program for typing and editing text. Its original function has been expanded to include other features such as tables, graphics, photos, or movie clips to support the content.

2. There are various applications of word processing in education for students and teachers.

3. From the hands-on activities, the following tasks were covered:
   - Basic word processing functions
     - Entering text
     - Checking spelling
     - Printing a document
     - Saving
       - Saving a document as you work
       - Saving a document with a different name (Using Save As)
   - Modifying text—inserting, selecting, deleting, moving, copying, and pasting
   - Formatting text—alignment, appearance, line spacing
   - Formatting the document
     - Selecting the page orientation
     - Adding a header or footer
     - Inserting page number
     - Having a different first page
     - Adding a clip art
     - Adding and deleting a page break
     - Changing margins
     - Indentation with the indentation markers
     - Working with tables
       - Adding
       - Formatting—borders and shading
       - Merging cells

Chapter 3

Graphic Tools and Page Design in Microsoft Office

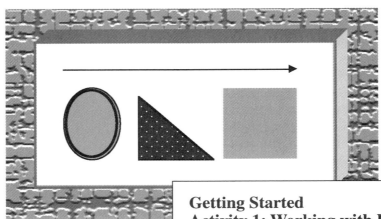

Getting Started
Activity 1: Working with Drawing
  Project 1
Activity 2: Grouping Objects in Drawing
  Project 2
Activity 3: Formatting a Picture
  Project 3
Activity 4: Creating a Page Layout
  Project 4
Activity 5: Creating a Web Page
  Project 5
Integration with Other Programs
Applications
Summary

Getting Started

 ## Features of Graphic Programs

Graphic programs can be classified into two categories: Drawing and Painting. The two programs—Drawing and Painting—have similarities as well as differences.

Drawing is an object-oriented graphic program in which the shapes are composed of **objects**. In Drawing it is not possible to delete part of the object (shape). For example, if you draw a circle, the circle itself is one unit. You cannot choose part of the circle. You may keep the circle or delete it. It is the same as the text in a word processing document. You can keep or delete a character such as a, b, c, but you cannot keep part of the character.

On the other hand, **Painting** is a bitmap graphic program in which the shapes are composed of **pixels**—small dots. Deleting some pixels from a shape is the same as erasing part of the shape. In Painting you can paint as if you are using crayons. Feel free to express your artistic style. Compared with Drawing, Painting files require much more space to save. If you are using a floppy disk, you may not have enough space to save a Painting file.

A Drawing program is good for precise drawings such as diagrams, logos, or high-contrast illustrations. A Painting program is good for digital paintings and photorealistic images. Particularly, it is good for freehand painting arts.

An object-oriented graphic program is available as a stand-alone program (e.g., Illustrator™, Free Hand™, Corel Draw™) or as part of integrated software (e.g., AppleWorks™) or as shared tools in a bundled software package (e.g., Microsoft Office™). Once you have learned how to use Drawing with any of these programs, you should be able to apply your knowledge to other Drawing programs. The Drawing program in AppleWorks™ and the drawing tools in MS Office™ are easy to use, while Illustrator™, Free Hand™, and Corel Draw™ are more complex and professional.

A bitmap graphic program is also available as a stand-alone program (e.g., Corel Painter™, PhotoShop™, KidPix™) or as part of integrated software, such as AppleWorks™. Once you have learned how to use the Painting tools with any of these programs, you should be able to apply your knowledge to other painting programs. PhotoShop™ is more complicated than AppleWorks™ Painting because it includes extensive image-editing functions. KidPix™ is a popular children's painting program.

Graphic Sources and Microsoft Office™

Graphic resources available in MS Office programs include drawing and some picture editing functions, but no painting. These graphic resources can be accessed from different MS Office programs—Word™, Excel™, or PowerPoint™. However, a graphic created in MS Office cannot be saved as a separate graphic file. Instead, it becomes part of the MS Office document that you are working on—Word™, Excel™, or PowerPoint™. The graphic resources in MS Office are not for creating graphics that need to be saved as different graphic formats, such as JPEG or GIF. However, the graphic can be copied and pasted into other application programs. Overall, the MS Office graphic resources have good features in drawing and picture editing.

In addition to creating graphics with drawing tools, a collection of ready-to-use clip arts is available. The clip arts can be drawing objects or photos. The clip arts can also be combined in the process of creating a graphic. For example, a food guide pyramid can be drawn with the drawing tools and then the clip arts for the food items can be inserted.

Another source of graphic is a chart created in spreadsheet, such as Excel™. A spreadsheet chart is the representation of the numerical data in a visual format, and it is the same as a drawing object.

 ## Graphic Programs in Teaching and Learning

Graphic programs can be used by both students and teachers. Following are a few examples of how students can use graphic programs:

- Supporting information and ideas
  - Students can illustrate the concepts in a drawing and insert that drawing in a research paper.
  - Students can draw organization charts and diagrams.

- Creative work
  - Students can draw floor plans (with Drawing tools).
  - Students can paint landscapes, portraits, or other themes (with Painting tools).

- Page layout
  - Students can create a newspaper.
  - Students can create invitation cards, notes, or flyers.

- Editing a scanned image
  - Students can edit the scanned image with Painting tools and photo editing tools.

- Presentation
  - Some graphic programs (e.g., AppleWorks™) give a presentation by creating a slide show.

Teachers can use graphic programs for instructional activities with the students' participation as indicated in the preceding examples. Also, teachers can use graphic programs for instructional material development and for classroom management:

- Instructional resource
  - Teachers can insert graphics in handouts or presentation materials.
  - Teachers can create flash cards.
  - Teachers can let the students—particularly younger students such as kindergartners—explore the Painting tools. Younger students enjoy painting better than drawing.
- Administrative use
  - Teachers can create a map to give directions for a field trip.
  - Teachers can create seating charts and classroom arrangement layouts.
  - Teachers can create name tags, certificates, signs, and flyers.
  - Teachers can insert graphics in reports or a presentation to the parents.

Overview of This Chapter

Activities and Projects

There are five activities that cover how to use Drawing tools and picture editing tools, and how to design a page layout and a web page. After each activity a project is provided to apply what was covered in the activity.

Applications, Integration with Other Programs, and Summary

At the end of the chapter, the Applications section can be used for brainstorming and developing ideas to use graphic tools in teaching and learning. Integration with Other Programs and Summary sections follow.

Icons to Watch

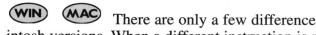 There are only a few differences between the Windows and Macintosh versions. When a different instruction is required, it is indicated by the corresponding icons.

 When there is a file on the CD that you can check, it is indicated with the icon.

More Information

MS Office does not have a separate graphic program, but the graphic tools are accessible from the programs in MS Office. Therefore, in this chapter, Word™ documents will be used to do the activities.

Activity 1: Working with a Drawing

This activity will show how to use graphic tools—Drawing Tools—in MS Office™.

This activity will guide you through the following tasks:

- Understanding the Drawing Tools in MS Office
- Drawing lines
- Selecting an object with the Select Objects Tool
- Deleting an object
- Moving an object
- Copying and pasting an object
- Drawing lines with different appearances: line weight, colors, and patterns
- Drawing squares and rectangles
- Filling in an object with color and effects
- Drawing objects with the Lines Tool
- Drawing objects with AutoShapes
- Adding and editing text
- Adding WordArt
- Creating a 3-D object
- Creating a shadowed object
- Formatting an object: Resizing manually
- Formatting an object: Rotating and flipping

> **CD** To browse the tasks that are covered in this activity by viewing a
> movie, check out the file **DrawingWin** (Windows) or **DrawingMac**
> (Macintosh) from the CD. (**Chapter 3** folder → **MoreInfo** folder →
> **DrawingWin** or **DrawingMac**)

Before You Begin

Create a new Word™ document.

Understanding the Drawing Tools in MS Office

The graphic tools—Drawing Tools—in MS Office can be accessed from the **View**
menu → **Toolbars** → **Drawing**. The Drawing Tools are used to draw different

shapes with different colors or patterns. Also, the graphic tools have picture editing functions. These tools are accessible from the MS Office programs such as Word™, Excel™, or PowerPoint™. However, it is not possible to save the graphic object or the edited picture as a separate graphic file.

Drawing Tools in Macintosh

Drawing Tools in Windows

You will explore the Drawing Tools in this activity. You begin with one page of a Word™ document. If you need more space add another page by inserting a page break. Make sure to keep the Drawing Tools on the screen (View menu → Toolbars → Drawing). The Drawing Tools may be shown vertically instead of horizontally.

 Drawing Lines

To draw a line, use the **Line Tool** ().

Let's draw a line:

1. Click the **Line Tool** once to select it, and then release the mouse. Is the Line Tool highlighted?

   You can draw shapes anywhere in the screen.

   As you click a drawing tool, a drawing area will be shown on the screen. Draw shapes inside this box. You can enlarge the box by dragging the corner of the box.

   > Create your drawing here.

2. Position the mouse on the screen in the location where you would like to draw a line.

3. Click the mouse and drag it until you finish a line, then release the mouse.

   ☐——————————☐

   Do you see the dots around the line? When a shape is drawn, dots will appear around the shape. This indicates that the shape (object) is selected. It is the same as selecting (highlighting) text in word processing. Then how do you unselect this shape? Click anywhere outside the shape!

4. Let's draw lines in different directions.

➡ ## Selecting an Object with the Select Objects Tool

To select an object (a shape) that you drew, use the **Select Objects Tool** ( ).

Let's select a line on the screen:

1. Choose the **Select Objects Tool**.
2. Click a line.

   Do you see dots around the line?

When you select a shape in Drawing, you can copy it, paste it, delete it, or move it to another location. The idea is the same as in word processing: copy and paste text, delete text, or move text (cut and paste text) to another location. The difference in the selection of the object is how it looks. In Drawing, the selected object has dots around the shape.

➡ ## Deleting an Object

Let's delete a line:

1. Select a line with the Select Objects Tool.
2. Press **Delete** (Macintosh) or **Backspace** (Windows) from the keyboard.

➡ ## Moving an Object

How about moving an object? Let's move a line to another location:

1. Click a line (any line) with the Select Objects Tool, and hold down the mouse.
2. Drag the mouse to a location where you would like to put the line, and then release the mouse.

➡ Copying and Pasting an Object

Let's copy and paste a line:

1. Select a line.
2. Choose **Copy** from the **Edit** menu.
3. Choose **Paste** from the **Edit** menu.
   Do you see another line? If not, drag the line. They may be overlaid.

➡ Drawing Lines with Different Appearances: Line Weight, Colors, and Patterns

You can draw lines with different colors, patterns, and thickness. The appearances of a line can be applied after the line is drawn. The following tools control the appearances of the line:

 Line Style Controls the line weight (thickness).

  Line Color Controls colors and patterns of a line.

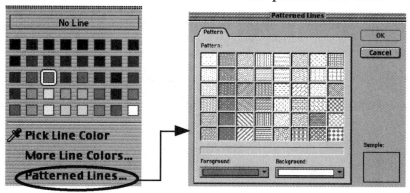

Let's draw a thick-patterned yellow line:

1. Draw a line with the Line Tool.

2. To change the line thickness:
   2-1. (While the line is selected) Click **Line Style** button.
   2-2. Choose a thick line.

3. To change the line color:
   3-1. (While the line is selected) Click **Line Color** button.
   3-2. Choose a color.

4. To change the line pattern:
   4-1. (While the line is selected) Click **Line Color**.
   4-2. In the Line Color window, choose **Patterned Lines**. It will bring the Patterned Lines options.
   4-3. Choose a pattern.
   4-4. Click **OK**.

Draw more lines with different appearances:

Drawing Rectangles and Squares

To draw rectangles or squares, use the **Rectangle** Tool ( ).

1. Choose the Rectangle Tool.

2. Click on the screen.
   A square appears surrounded with dots.

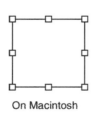
On Macintosh

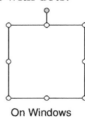
On Windows

The pointed line with the green dot on Windows is for free rotate. Free rotate will be discussed later. To rotate the object, click the green dot and rotate it.

3. To change the size or to make it a rectangle, click one of the dots, hold it, drag it, and then release the mouse.

Draw a few rectangles and squares:

Draw rectangles and squares with various patterns and colors of lines.

Filling in an Object with Color and Effects

It is possible to fill in an object with color, gradient, texture, pattern, and even a picture. The color and effects can be filled in any closed objects—rectangles, circles, triangles, polygons, and irregular shapes. Filling in options are in the **Fill Color** Tool.

 Fill Color Controls filling-in color, pattern, and shadow.

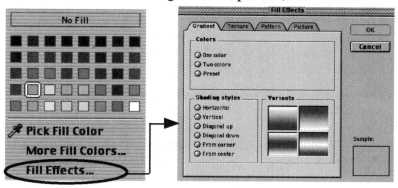

Let's draw rectangles with different colors, patterns, textures, and gradients.

1. Draw a rectangle.

2. To fill in the color:
   2-1. (While the line is selected) Click **Fill Color** tool.
   2-2. Choose the color.

3. To fill in the gradient, texture, and/or pattern:
   3-1. (While the line is selected) Click **Fill Color** tool.
   3-2. In the Fill Color window, choose **Fill Effects**.
       It will bring the Fill Effects options.
   3-3. Choose a tab.

   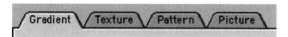

   NOTE Picture can be filled in if you have a picture saved in a separate file.
   3-4. Explore and choose the effect.
   3-5. Click **OK**.

Drawing Objects with the Lines Tool

More line tools are available besides the simple straight line. These tools are in the **Lines Tool**. On Windows, from the Drawing Toolbar, choose **AutoShapes → Lines Tool**. On Macintosh, the Lines Tool is in the Drawing Toolbar.

 Lines Tool

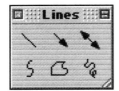

     Arrowheads: To draw arrowheads.

     Scribble: To draw lines as if using a pencil.

     Freeform: To draw a shape with angles.

     Curve: To draw irregular curved shapes. It is similar to the Freeform Tool, but the difference is in creating curved shapes instead of angled ones.

Let's draw lines with arrowheads (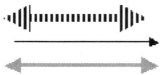). Add different thicknesses and colors.

> **NOTE**   More arrow formats are available from the **Arrow Style**. On Windows, Arrow Style is on the Drawing Toolbar. On Macintosh, from the Drawing Toolbar, choose Draw Tool → Arrow Style. To use these arrow styles, draw a line and then apply the style.

 Arrow Style

Let's draw objects with Scribble (). Again, on Windows, choose AutoShapes → Lines Tool.

Let's draw objects with Freeform (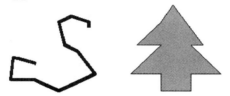).

1. Click the Freeform Tool.
2. Click where you want the first point of the shape to appear.
3. Move the cursor and click where you want the next point.
4. To finish the curved shape, double-click where you want the last point to appear.

Let's draw an irregular curved shape with Curve (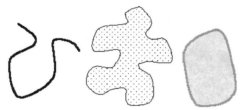). Drawing a shape with the Curve Tool is the same as the Freeform Tool.

Drawing Objects with AutoShapes

AutoShapes is a collection of objects that are commonly used shapes. AutoShapes has several categories. Drawing objects by using these shapes is the same as drawing a line or a rectangle.

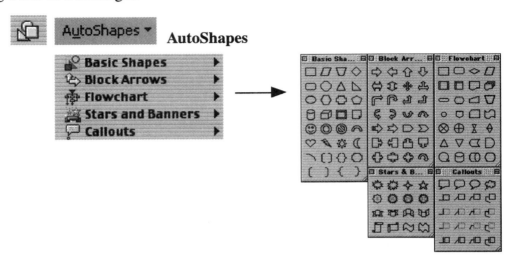

Draw several objects by using AutoShapes. Use different colors and effects for the lines and filling in. The following are a few examples:

 ## Adding and Editing Text

Text Box Tool is used to type text as if you are using a word processing program. You can choose different fonts, sizes, and styles. But the difference is that the text created with the drawing tool is considered a drawing object instead of text such as in a word processing document.

  Text Box

Let's type text.

1. Choose the Text Box.

2. Click where you want to locate the Text Box on the screen.

The text box appears with the blinking cursor (text insertion point) inside:

3. Type something.

4. The text appearance—font, size, style, and color—can be changed with the same menu and the tool bar as in Word™. You can choose different text colors from the **Font Color** Tool, which is available both in the Drawing Tool and Formatting Tool.

5. When finished, click anywhere outside the box.
   The text box can be filled in with color or pattern like a rectangle.

   NOTE   If the box size should be adjusted, click one of the dots in the box and drag it. To select the box, use the Select Objects Tool. If you don't want to see the box around the text, choose white color from the Line Color Tool.

➡ Adding WordArt

WordArt is a preformatted and designed text. It is useful to add a special effect in the presentation and page layout. WordArt can be added by using the **Insert WordArt** Tool.

Let's add WordArt.

1. Choose the Insert WordArt Tool.
   The WordArt Gallery appears:

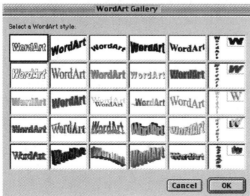

2. Choose a style in one of the following ways:
   * Clicking it once and click **OK**.
   * Double-clicking it.

   Edit WordArt Text dialog box appears:

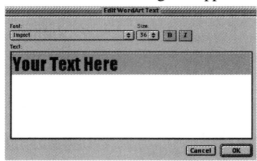

3. Type your text.

4. Click **OK**.
   Stretch the text, if necessary.

Creating a 3-D Object

A two-dimensional object can be transformed into a three-dimensional (3-D) object. Use **3-D Style**. On Windows, 3-D is in the Drawing Toolbar. On Macintosh, from the Drawing Toolbar choose Draw → 3-D.

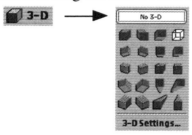

Let's draw a 3-D object.

1. Draw any closed object—rectangle, circle, triangle, or an irregular shape.

2. Select the object, if not selected.

3. Choose 3-D, then choose a 3-D style.

Try different 3-D objects. The following are a few examples:

Creating a Shadowed Object

A shadow effect can be added to a closed shape. Use **Shadow Style**. On Windows, Shadow Style is in the Drawing Toolbar. On Macintosh, from the Drawing Toolbar, choose Draw → Shadow.

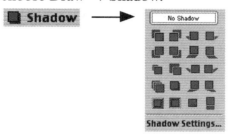

Draw objects with shadow.

Formatting an Object: Resizing Manually

It is possible to resize an object manually. Let's resize an object:

1. Select an object with the Select Objects Tool.
2. Drag one of the dots to the direction that you want to go—to make it smaller or bigger.

Formatting an Object: Rotating and Flipping

The graphic objects can be formatted by rotating and flipping them. Rotating and flipping functions are in the **Drawing Toolbar** → **Draw Tool** → choose **Rotate and Flip**. These rotating and flipping functions may not be applied to some clip arts.

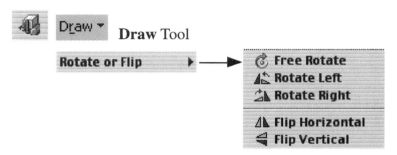

To make any changes to an object:

1. Select an object.
2. Choose one of the options shown in the **Rotate and Flip** options. Do experiments.

Try all the options: Free Rotate, Rotate Left, Rotate Right, Flip Horizontal, and Flip Vertical.

Finishing Touches

Save the file as DRAWING1.

Project 1

Project 1 is to draw and format the shapes with the drawing tools.

1. Create a new Word™ document.

2. Draw the following shapes:

3. Draw the shapes and transform them:

   3-1.

   3-2.

   3-3.

   3-4.

4. Type text with WordArt and Text Box.

5. Save the document as **DR1**.

Activity 2: Grouping Objects in a Drawing

In Activity 1, the use of Drawing Tools was discussed. This activity is based on the following scenario to create a diagram using the Drawing Tools:

> "Students in Group 1 finished a report about computer hardware. Now they want to add a diagram describing how these computer hardware components are working together to process information."

This activity will guide you through the following tasks:

- Moving objects to the front or to the back
- Selecting multiple objects
- Grouping objects
- Making changes to the grouped object
- Ungrouping the object

Before You Begin

Create a new Word™ document.

Moving Objects to the Front or to the Back

When you have an object laid on top of another, you can move it to the back or to the front. Let's have a text and a box, and then make sure that the text is on top of the box. The function for moving objects to the front or back is in the Draw Tool. On Windows, Draw Tool → **Order**. On Macintosh, Draw Tool → **Arrange**.

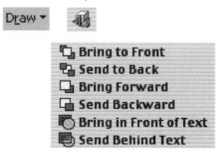

Let's send an object to back.

1. Type **CPU** with the Text Box (A).

2. Draw a rectangle on top of the word CPU.
   You may not see the text because it is hidden underneath the rectangle.

3. While the rectangle is selected, choose Draw Tool → **Arrange** or
   Order → Send to Back.
   The rectangle will be sent to the back of the text. (The rectangle and the
   text changed the sequence of the layers.)

Draw the following diagram.

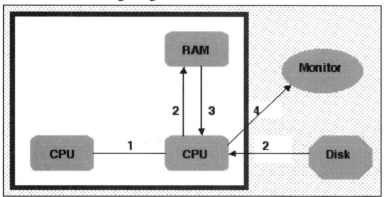

➡ Selecting Multiple Objects

To select one object, you can click the object with the Select Objects Tool ( ).
What if you need to select more than one object? There are two ways:

   a. Using the Select Objects Tool and Shift key.
   b. Using the Select Objects Tool to define the selection area.

Let's select the objects using the **Select Objects** Tool and **Shift key:**

1. Choose the Select Objects Tool.
2. Click an object that you want to select.
   Do you see the dots around it?
3. Hold down the **Shift** key from the keyboard.
4. While holding down the **Shift** key, click another object with the Select
   Objects Tool.
   Do you have two objects selected?
5. While holding down the **Shift** key, click one more object with the Select
   Objects Tool.
   Do you have three objects selected?
   This is how to select several objects manually.

Let's unselect what you have selected:

1. Release the Shift key.
2. Click anywhere outside the objects.
   The dots around the objects will disappear.

Let's select objects with the **Select Objects** Tool to define the selection area:

1. Choose the Select Objects Tool.
2. With the Select Objects Tool, draw a rectangle around the objects that you want to select. (This is not drawing a rectangle with the Rectangle Tool.)

Do you see the dots around the objects?

➡ Grouping Objects

Your drawing is composed of several objects. You can combine them and make one object instead of having multiple objects. The function for grouping is available in the Draw Tool.

Let's group the objects that you drew.

1. Select the objects as follows:

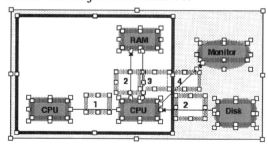

2. Choose **Draw** Tool → **Group**.

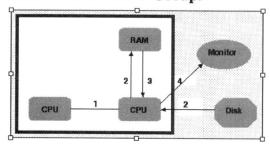

All the objects became one unit, and this process is called **grouping**. Grouping does not change the size of the objects, it simply makes one object.

 ## Making Changes to the Grouped Object

Copy and Paste the grouped object before making changes to it.

You have two identical objects. If you don't see two objects, drag the one that you see. The other must be underneath.

Because the objects are grouped, any changes will affect the whole object. Let's make the line thicker on the **second** object:

1. Select the second object.
2. Make the line thicker.
   Did you notice that all the lines in the object have been changed?

 ## Ungrouping the Object

Ungrouping is unlocking the grouped object to make individual objects. The function for ungrouping is available in the Draw Tool.

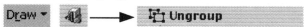

Let's ungroup the second object that has thicker lines.

1. Click the second object.
2. Choose **Draw** Tool → **Ungroup**.
   Do you see dots around each object?
3. Click anywhere outside the objects.
   No dots shown? That means no object is selected.

Finishing Touches

Save the document as DRAWING2.

Project 2

Project 2 is to draw the Food Guide Pyramid using the drawing tools.

1. Create a new Word™ document.
2. Create the Food Guide Pyramid with the drawing tools. The outline of the Food Guide Pyramid is shown in the following diagram. See the instructions below for the format.

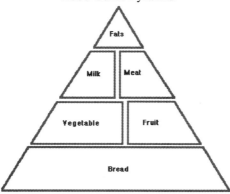

Food Guide Pyramid

- Each food group should be one object. Choose appropriate drawing tools to draw.

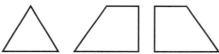

- Apply various styles and effects to the objects.
- Use WordArt for the title `Food Guide Pyramid`.
- Use Text Box for the title of each food group.

3. Group the objects. (Group all the objects into one unit.)
4. Draw the background—a box around the pyramid.
5. Save the document as **DR2**.

> (CD) To see a finished sample project, check out the file **DR-Proj2** from the CD. (**Chapter 3** folder → **Projects** folder → **DR-Proj2**)

Activity 3: Formatting a Picture

This activity is a lesson on how to format pictures in MS Office™.

This activity will guide you through the following tasks:

- Understanding the sources of pictures
- Getting the picture formatting tools
- Color control
- Filling color and effects
- Brightness and Contrast
- Picture Effects
- Cropping a picture with Crop Tool
- Cropping a picture with Marquees and Lassos

Before You Begin

Create a new Word™ document.

 ## Understanding the Sources of Pictures

The sources of pictures that you can use in an MS Office document are clip arts from MS Office, separate graphic or photo files, or images directly imported from a scanner or a digital camera. The picture formatting techniques that you will explore in this activity can be applied to most types of pictures, although some techniques may not work on some drawing objects. The clip arts from MS Office can be drawing objects or pictures.

Insert a clip art of a photo.

NOTE On Macintosh, to access the full list of clip arts and photos, the Value Pack should be installed on the hard drive from the MS Office program CD.

Throughout the activity, the following graphic will be used as an example. In your file, use the photo that you inserted.

Let's have six sets of the picture as in the following figure, so that you can compare different effects easily. Copy and paste the picture. To leave space between the pictures, press Tab. When it goes down to the next line, make sure to leave a blank line between the pictures.

 Getting the Picture Formatting Tools

Picture formatting tools are in the **View** menu:

    a. **View** menu → **Toolbars** → **Picture**
    b. **View** menu → **Formatting Palette** (only on Macintosh)

Let's show the picture formatting tools:

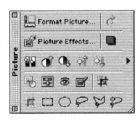

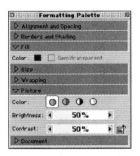

The picture formatting options that we will use in the Formatting Palette are Fill and Picture. These options will be shown in the palette when a picture is selected. The Formatting Palette allows an easy access to the options that are listed from the Picture Toolbar → Format Picture.

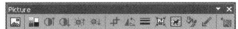

Although the Windows version does not have the Formatting Palette, the similar functions can be accessed from the Picture Toolbar → Format Picture. Therefore, in the following instructions, when it is indicated as Formatting Palette, you know how to access it.

Color Control

Color Control is to change the color attributes of the picture: Automatic (Original), Grayscale, Black & White, and Watermark/Washout.

Picture Toolbar

Formatting Palette

Let's apply color attributes. Try all four options—Automatic, Grayscale, Black & White, and Watermark/Washout. You can use four pictures.

1. Select one picture by clicking it.
2. Choose the **Color Control**—Automatic, Grayscale, Watermark, or Black & White.

 ## Filling Color and Effects

Filling color and effects is used to fill in color, gradient, texture, pattern, and even a picture as the background of the picture. It also has an option to make filling in the color and semitransparent effects.

Filling Color and Effects can be accessed from the **Picture Toolbar → Format Picture → Colors and Lines** tab.

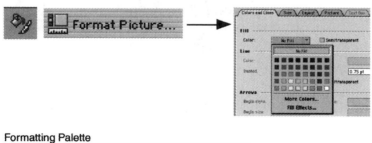

Formatting Palette

To see the filling color and effects, the graphic should have room for the background. If your photo is a complete photo, insert a clip art or a photo that you can fill in the background. If necessary, insert another clip art.

Let's fill color (and/or gradient, texture, pattern) with the semitransparent option. Filling in color and effects can be applied even to the pictures that you transformed into different color attributes—grayscale, black & white, or watermark/washout.

1. Select a picture.
2. From the Picture Toolbar choose **Format Picture → Colors and Lines** tab. (Or click the **Color** box from the Formatting Palette on Macintosh).
3. Choose a color.

4. Let's add the semitransparent effect.

 **(MS Office 2001)**
While the picture is selected, click the **Semitransparent** box.

 **(MS Office v.X)**
Adjust the **Transparency** Bar.

NOTE   For filling in effects, select **Fill Effects** from the Color palette. This is the same as filling in colors and effects in an object in Activity 1. When you use the effects, you may not be able to use the semitransparent option.

➡ Brightness and Contrast

Brightness controls how dark or light the picture is. **Contrast** controls how sharply distinctive the elements in the picture are. Often when the elements of the picture are dramatically dark and light, it gives more contrast.

Let's change the appearance of the photo by increasing or decreasing the brightness or contrast.

1. Select a picture.

2. Increase (or decrease) the brightness (or contrast).

Picture Effects

Picture Effects add a special effect to the picture. The Picture Effects function is available only on Macintosh. To use Picture Effects, it should be a picture from a graphic file such as JPEG, GIF, and so on. Picture Effects may not be applied to some drawing objects.

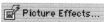

Let's apply picture effects:

1. Select a picture.

2. Click **Picture Effects** from the Picture Toolbar.
   The Effects Gallery appears:

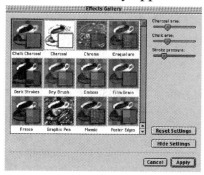

3. Select an effect by clicking it.

4. Click **Apply**. The following are a few examples:

 Cropping a Picture with the Crop Tool

Cropping a Picture is to select a part of the picture and keep it. It is different from changing the picture size to smaller. When you change the picture size to smaller, the whole picture becomes smaller proportionally. When you crop the picture, you can eliminate an unwanted part of the picture. One way of cropping is using the **Crop** Tool from the Picture Toolbar.

Let's crop a picture.

1. Select a picture.

2. Select the **Crop** Tool from the Picture Toolbar.

3. Click the dot with the Crop Tool, and drag it toward inside the picture.

Crop Tool

4. Crop all the corners of the picture, as you need.

Cropping a Picture with Marquees and Lassos

Marquees and **Lassos** are the selection tools used to select part of the picture. Marquees and Lassos are available only on Macintosh. With the combination of the Cut Out Tool, you can select and crop a picture in different shapes. Use Marquees to select a regular rectangle or oval shape, and Lassos to select an irregular shape.

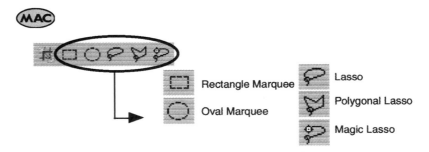

Rectangle Marquee

Oval Marquee

Lasso

Polygonal Lasso

Magic Lasso

Let's crop a picture.

1. Select a picture.

2. Select a Marquee or a Lasso.

3. Draw the boundary of the picture that you want to keep.

Boundary in the dotted line

4. Click the **Cut Out** Tool.

Cut Out Tool

Only the selected area will remain.

Finishing Touches

Save the file as DRAWING3.

Project 3

This project is to find clip arts or pictures that you can use for the Food Guide Pyramid page layout, and then format them.

1. Create a new Word™ document.
2. Insert clip arts or pictures that you can use for the Food Guide Pyramid page layout—ideally, one for each food group. (If you can't find them all, get at least a couple.)
3. Copy and paste the clip art or picture to be formatted. You may need several sets—at least five.
4. When you format the clip art or picture, indicate which technique is used. The following are the formatting techniques to be used. (You can use Text Box next to the clip art and type the technique used.)
   - Color control—Grayscale
   - Color control—Watermark/Washout
   - Filling color or effects
   - Brightness and Contrast control
   - Cropping the picture
   - (Macintosh only) Cropping the picture using a Marquee or Lasso
   - (Macintosh only) Applying Picture Effects
5. Save the file as **DR3**.

Activity 4: Creating a Page Layout

In this activity the graphic and text will be combined to create a page layout.

"Group 1 created a diagram in DRAWING2 on how the information flows in the computer hardware components. Earlier they created the file WORD4 to describe the components of computer hardware. Now they want to create a newsletter-type page layout with these two files."

Files needed for this activity: WORD4 and DRAWING2

This activity will guide you through the following tasks:

- Making multiple columns
- Wrapping text: WordArt in line with text
- Wrapping text: Graphic as a background
- Wrapping text: Graphic around the text

Before You Begin

1. Let's prepare the file WORD4.
   - 1-1. Open the file WORD4.
   - 1-2. Save WORD4 as WORD5.
   - 1-3. Delete the title `Report: Computer Hardware` in page 1.
   - 1-4. Delete the text indicated as **1.4 Delete the text** in the following figure.
   - 1-5. Do not indent the first line of the paragraph as indicated in the following figure, **1.5**. Delete the tab indentation. (It is possible that you may have to move the indentation markers to delete the indentation.)

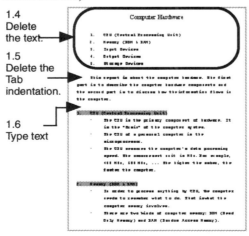

1-6. Type the following text using 18 point Bold before the subtitle
`1. CPU (Central Processing Unit)`, as marked in the
previous figure:

`Computer Hardware Components`

1-7. In the header, make the font size smaller—choose 10 point.

1-8. Delete the page break between pages 1 and 2.
If the paragraph below the student names becomes the center
alignment, change it back to the left alignment.

1-9. At the end of the document, leave a blank line and add the
following title using 18 point Bold without indentation:

`The Information Flow`

1-10. Below the title `The Information Flow`, type the following
text using 12 point plain text (use the tab key to leave space after
the number and period.):

`1. CPU reads instruction from ROM (and/or System`
`software).`

`2. CPU copies a file from the disk and stores it`
`in RAM.`

`3. CPU takes the information from RAM.`

`4. CPU displays the information on the monitor.`

1-11. Change the line spacing of the whole document to Single spacing.
(Select the whole document. For line spacing changes, choose
Format menu → Paragraph.)

The file should be similar in appearance to the following figure.
(You may not see the exact ending of the pages.)

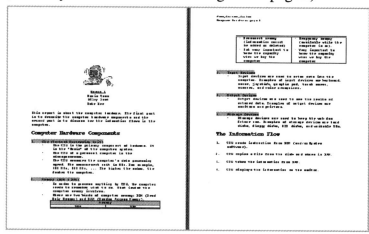

2. Open the file DRAWING2.

Making Multiple Columns

So far we have used the single column. The single column is the default in a word processing program, and usually we use the single-column format. Yet, it is possible to use multiple columns—two columns or more.

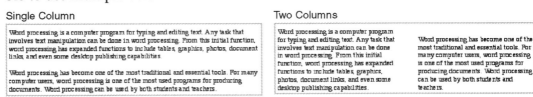

Single Column

Word processing is a computer program for typing and editing text. Any task that involves text manipulation can be done in word processing. From this initial function, word processing has expanded functions to include tables, graphics, photos, document links, and even some desktop publishing capabilities.

Word processing has become one of the most traditional and essential tools. For many computer users, word processing is one of the most used programs for producing documents. Word processing can be used by both students and teachers.

Two Columns

Word processing is a computer program for typing and editing text. Any task that involves text manipulation can be done in word processing. From this initial function, word processing has expanded functions to include tables, graphics, photos, document links, and even some desktop publishing capabilities.

Word processing has become one of the most traditional and essential tools. For many computer users, word processing is one of the most used programs for producing documents. Word processing can be used by both students and teachers.

Let's make 2 Columns for the text under the subtitle `1. CPU (Central Processing Unit)`.

1. Select the text to make 2 Columns as indicated in the following figure:

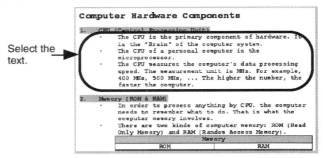

Select the text.

2. Click **Columns** button from the Standard Toolbar.

Columns

3. Choose **2 Columns**.
   The text will be transformed into two columns.

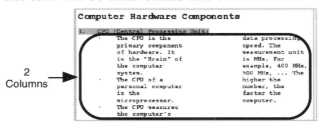

2 Columns

Let's format the hanging indent for the two-columned text. Currently, it is 0.5-inch indentation. Make it 0.25 inch to reduce the redundant space.

1. Select the text—two-columned text. Make sure to select both columns.
2. Move the indentation markers to make 0.25-inch indentation.

Change the text under each subtitle to two-columned text and format the hanging indent to 0.25 inch. Do not touch the table under subtitle 2. `Memory (ROM & RAM)`. When you finish, it should be similar to the following figure:

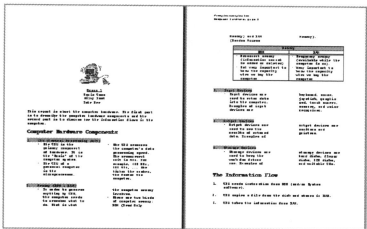

NOTE You may have noticed that the table is not aligned with the text anymore because the hanging indent has been changed. So change the size of the table by dragging the line. When you drag the line for one column, the size of the columns may not be even. Then, you can adjust the line between columns as well.

Memory	
ROM	**RAM**
· Permanent memory (information cannot be added or deleted) · Not very important to	· Temporary memory (available while the computer is on) · Very important to

Adjust the table size.

Wrapping Text: WordArt in Line with Text

Wrapping text is to arrange the text in relationship to a graphic. It could be putting the text behind the graphic, in front of the graphic, in line with the graphic, or surrounding the graphic.

Let's add the title `Computer Hardware` with WordArt and line up with the text.

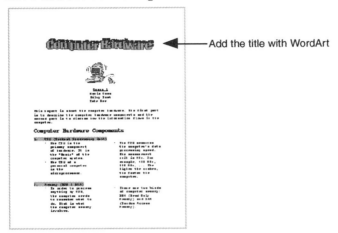

Add the title with WordArt

1. Click in the very beginning of page 1. That is where WordArt will be placed.

2. Create a WordArt.
   (In this example, 28-point text was selected.)
   The WordArt toolbar appears. If not, click WordArt.

3. Click **Text Wrapping** icon, then select **In Line with Text**.

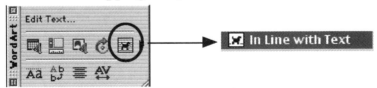

   In Line with Text means that WordArt will be like a regular text in word processing.

4. Put the title in the right place.
   4-1.   If there are extra spaces before the WordArt title, delete them.
   4-2.   Stretch WordArt to make a visible headline.

Wrapping Text: Graphic as a Background

It is possible to place a graphic as a background. Let's use the graphic that you inserted as the background.

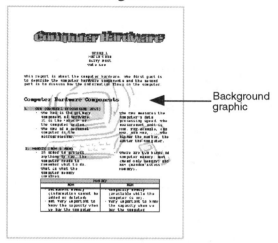

Background graphic

1. Click the computer graphic.

2. Enlarge the graphic.

3. Make the graphic as Watermark/Washout.
   (Watermark/Washout was chosen because the background graphic should not be too distinctive and the Watermark/Washout option lightens the graphic significantly.)

4. Let's choose Text Wrapping Style—Behind Text.

   While the graphic is selected, from the **Formatting Palette** choose **Wrapping → Behind Text**.

   While the graphic is selected, from the **Picture Toolbar** choose **Text Wrapping button → Behind Text**.

5. Drag the graphic to the proper location.

NOTE   Printing a document with the graphic behind the text works well in the Windows version XP and Macintosh v.X, but not in Macintosh version 2001. In Macintosh version 2001, the graphic will be printed on top of the text.

Wrapping Text: Graphic around the Text

The graphic can be wrapped around the text. In this section, you will insert the graphic that you created in DRAWING2—the information flow in the computer hardware components.

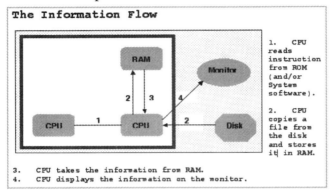

1. From DRAWING2 file, copy the graphic.

2. In WORD5 click below the title `The Information Flow`.

3. Paste the graphic.

4. Let's choose Text Wrapping Style—Square.

While the graphic is selected, from the **Formatting Palette** choose **Wrapping → Square**.

4-1. Double-click the graphic.
    Format Object dialog box appears.

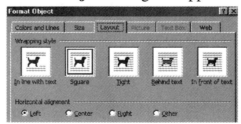

4-2. In the dialog box, choose **Layout** tab.
If this tab is not available, the grouped object was not selected properly. Only a component inside the grouped object may have been selected. Click anywhere outside the graphic not to select it. And then double-click the graphic again. Sometimes it doesn't seem to select the grouped object properly. If that is the case, just try a few times.

4-3. From the Layout tab choose **Square** for the Wrapping Style.

4-4. From the Layout tab choose **Left** for the Horizontal Alignment.

5. Drag the graphic in the right place, below the title `The Information Flow`. You may have to try several times to get the right spot.

If it is necessary to reduce the size of the graphic, do so. But be careful because the text may become invisible.

Finishing Touches

1. Change the margin if the newsletter goes to page 3, particularly because the table did not fit in page 1.

Format menu → Document.

File menu → Page Setup.
(Do not select the graphic. If you are selecting the graphic, the Page Setup may not be available.)

2. Save the file.

Project 4

This project is to create a page layout about the Food Guide Pyramid.

1. Create a 2-3 page newsletter-type layout about the Food Guide Pyramid. You can use the files **WP4**, **DR2**, and **DR3**. Include the following:
   - 2-Column text
   - At least two different Text wrapping styles
   - Clip arts or pictures formatted with the picture formatting tools
2. Save the file as **DR4**.

Activity 5: Creating a Web Page

In Activity 5, a Web page will be created based on the page layout from Activity 4.

File needed for this activity: WORD5

This activity will guide you through the following tasks:

- Planning a Web page
- Preparing the text
- Adding bookmarks
- Inserting hyperlinks
- Completing the links
- Previewing the Web page
- Saving as Web page

Before You Begin

1. Open WORD5.

2. Save the file as WORD6.

 ## Planning a Web Page

When you create a Web page, it is necessary to plan the navigation of the information. In this activity, you will have two options in the beginning of the page to go to either Computer Hardware Components or The Information Flow. After visiting the links there will be an option to go back to the top of the document.

> **CD** To see the finished sample file, check out the file **Word6** and **Web.htm** from the CD. (**Chapter 3** folder → **MoreInfo** folder)

Preparing the Text

Type
- `Computer Hardware Components`
- `The Information Flow`

as in the following figure:
(Make sure to have a single column.)

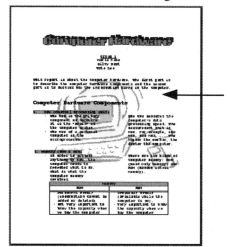
- `Computer Hardware Components`
- `The Information Flow`

 Adding Bookmarks

A **bookmark** is to indicate a specific location to link the information in the Web. In this activity, the text added in the previous section will be linked to the locations—`Computer Hardware Components` and `The Information Flow`.

Let's add a bookmark in the section of `Computer Hardware Components`.

1. Click in front of the title `Computer Hardware Components`.

2. Choose **Bookmark. . .** from the **Insert** menu.

3. Enter bookmark name:
   3-1. In the dialog box, enter the bookmark name. In this example, it is
   `Hardware`.

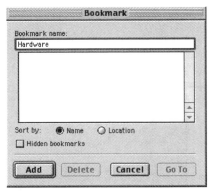

3-2. Click **Add**.

Add a bookmark in the section of `The Information Flow`. **The**
bookmark name is `Information`.

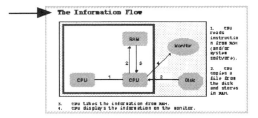

Inserting Hyperlinks

A **hyperlink** is to link the elements of the page to the specified location. In this activity the text will be linked to the bookmarks as follows:

Text	Bookmark
• `Computer Hardware Components`	`Hardware`
• `The Information Flow`	`Information`

Let's link the text, • `Computer Hardware Components` to the bookmark
Hardware.

1. Select the text, • `Computer Hardware Components`.

2. Choose **Hyperlink. . .** from the **Insert** menu.

3. Let's select the bookmark.

    3-1. Choose the **Document** tab (because the bookmark is in the document).

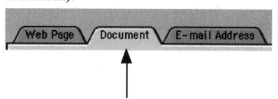

    3-2. Click **Locate** button.

    3-3. Select the bookmark **Hardware**.

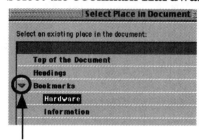

    3-4. Click **OK**.

        The bookmark name will appear in the anchor box.

    3-5. Click **OK**.

        The link is created. The text has changed its color and is underlined.

    3-1. Click **Place in This Document**.

    3-2. Select the bookmark **Hardware**.

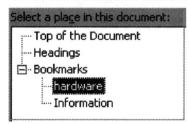

    3-3. Click **OK**.

Link the text, • The Information Flow to the bookmark **Information**.

Test the links by clicking the hyperlinked text. To test the links, choose **Web Page Preview** from the **File** menu. It will open an Internet browser. On Macintosh, you can also click the hyperlink without choosing the web page preview option. Does it go to the bookmarked location?

NOTE   On Macintosh, if you need to revise the hyperlink, hold down the Control key and then click the hyperlinked text. From the pop-up menu, choose **Hyperlink** → **Edit Hyperlink**.

 ## Completing the Links

So far the hyperlinks are created to go to the bookmarks. Now, there should be a way to come back to the top of the document after visiting the bookmarked location.

Let's add text **Back** at the end of the Computer Hardware Components section, to go back to the beginning of the document.

1. Type **Back** at the end of the Computer Hardware Components section.

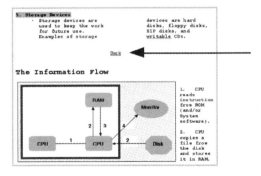

2. Select the text Back.

3. Choose **Hyperlink. . .** from the **Insert** menu.
   For detailed instructions, refer to the section Inserting Hyperlinks. To link to the top of the document, select **Top of the Document**.

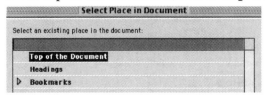

Copy the text **Back**, and paste it at the end of `The Information Flow` section, to go back to the beginning of the document. (Because the text has hyperlink, you can use the same hyperlink in another location.)

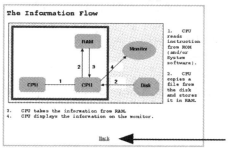

Test the links.

Previewing the Web Page

You can preview the Web page. To preview the Web page, Choose **Web Page Preview** from the **File** menu. This will prompt the default Internet browser.

Saving as a Web Page

You can save this word processing file as Web Page—html file.

Before saving the presentation as Web Page, save the current file.

Let's save the file as Web Page:

1. Choose **Save As Web Page. . .** from the **File** menu.

2. Give the file name as **Web.htm**, and choose the file format as **Web Page**.

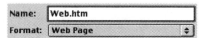

The file titled **Web.htm** will be created, along with the folder **Web_files**. The folder contains all the necessary files.

Web.htm   Web_files

3. To view the Web page, open the file **Web.htm** from an Internet browser program, usually by choosing Open from the File menu.

The Web page may be viewed differently depending on the Internet browser.

Project 5

This project is to create a Web page about the Food Guide Pyramid.

1. Create a Web page based on the file DR4.
   - Create bookmarks
   - Create hyperlinks
   - Complete the links to go back and forth between the hyperlinks and the bookmarks.
2. Save the file as **DR5**.
3. Save the file as Web Page. File name is **DR5Web.htm**.

Integration with Other Programs

The major role of graphic use is to promote understanding for the learners. Diagrams, charts, or concept maps can be created to illustrate the topics and contents. Also, pictures can be used for a realistic portrayal of objects. Often, the graphic can be used to enhance the appearance of the document or presentation.

Integration of graphic programs with other application programs is the most common arrangement. The graphic can be drawing objects, painting, clip arts, scanned pictures, or digital photos from a digital camera. The graphic can be inserted literally anywhere—in word processing, presentation, Web page, database, and even in spreadsheet. Because the potential and the possibilities of using the graphic programs with other application programs are endless, the creative ideas from such integration can be endless as well.

Applications

In this chapter, the drawing and picture formatting techniques and the ideas for using graphic tools in the classroom were discussed. Examine the possibilities of applying graphic tools in education.

1. Collect ideas on how to use graphic tools with the students. You can refer to the section *Getting Started* to create your own ideas. Consider the following example to get started:

Example

Activity Purpose: To record the growing plants project.
Activity Description: Students can plant seeds in three pots, then place them in different locations—sunny outdoor, sunny window sill, and shady outdoor—and record the growth of the plants regularly. Students can take photos of the plants once a week with a ruler next to the plant to show the growth. And then, they can format the photos to use for the report. For example, a photo can be cropped to keep only the necessary part. The prepared photos can be arranged for the same cluster and then grouped as one unit (grouping objects in drawing). Students can also use other drawing tools to enhance the report. The report can be regular paper style or newsletter style with multiple columns and text wrapping around the graphic. Also, the report can be saved as a Web page. (If the plant growth record is kept in a spreadsheet, students can also create a chart and use it in the report.)

---

2. Collect ideas on how to use graphic tools as a teacher for classroom management and teaching. You can refer to the section *Getting Started* to create your own ideas.

3. Create a lesson plan in which you can integrate graphic tools by expanding the ideas in the section *Getting Started* or by developing your own ideas. Include the following components:
   • Subject matter
   • Grade level
   • Purpose of the activity (lesson objective)
   • Target audience
     • Prior knowledge on the lesson objective (any related content covered?)
     • Computer skill
     • Any other information that you want to include

- Environment
  - Location: In the classroom or in the lab?
  - Number of computers needed
- Description of instructional activity
  - Description on how the lesson will proceed and how Drawing will be used

4. Collect ideas on how to integrate graphics with other programs. You can refer to the section *Integration with Other Programs* to create your own ideas.

Summary

1. Microsoft Office™ has graphic tools for drawing and picture formatting that are easy to use and useful. These graphic tools can be accessed from the MS Office programs—for example, Word™, Excel™, or PowerPoint™. The graphic created in MS Office cannot be saved as a separate graphic file, but it can be copied and pasted into other files.

2. From the Drawing hands-on activities, the following tasks were covered:
   - Drawing different shapes (objects)—lines, rectangles, AutoShapes, curves, free forms, WordArt, Text Box, 3-D, and shadowed objects
   - Drawing shapes with different appearances—line weight, colors, and patterns
   - Formatting shapes—moving, deleting, copying, resizing, rotating, and flipping
   - Grouping and ungrouping objects
   - Formatting pictures—Color control, Brightness and Contrast, Picture Effects, Cropping
   - Page layouts—multiple columns, wrapping text styles
   - Creating a web page

Chapter 4

Microsoft Excel: The Spreadsheet Tool

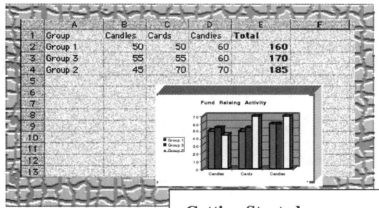

Getting Started
Activity 1: Working with Spreadsheet
  Project 1
Activity 2: Using Spreadsheet
        Features I
  Project 2
Activity 3: Using Spreadsheet
        Features II
  Project 3
Integration with Other Programs
Applications
Summary

Getting Started

 Features of a Spreadsheet

Spreadsheet is a computer program for calculating and manipulating numerical data. Spreadsheet is composed of rows and columns. Unlike a word processing program that starts with one blank page, a new spreadsheet document has many pages of rows and columns.

The features of spreadsheet programs can be summarized as follows:

- **Calculation**. This is the most important function in spreadsheet. In addition to adding, subtracting, multiplying, and dividing, specified formula could calculate mathematical equations. Also, common tasks—such as calculating total or average and finding the lowest or highest value—can be accomplished by inserting the functions to calculate. As an advanced application, a specific value can be defined and assigned to the corresponding entry. For example, you can define the temperature in three ranges—above 90 degrees as "hot," 75–90 degrees as "warm," and 60–75 degrees as "cool"—and then have these values entered in the spreadsheet.

- **Efficiency in data entry**. When the data are repeated, they can be entered at the same time in the selected cells—for example, to enter the value "80" in 10 consecutive cells. This efficiency of data entry is even more powerful when you use the functions. For example, when there are 100 cells to calculate average, only the first cell needs to be calculated. The remaining 99 cells can be filled in from the first cell. By doing this, a large amount of data can be calculated fast.

- **Sorting data**. The data in spreadsheet can be sorted in any order—ascending or descending. For example, the data can be sorted by ascending order of the last names or by descending order of average.

- **Charts**. Transforming numerical data into a chart is a strong visual presentation. Modern spreadsheet programs have abundant options for charts—not only different types of charts (bar, pie, line, etc.) but also different appearances (regular, 3-D).

- **Automatic recalculation**. When a value changes in the spreadsheet, the corresponding values will be recalculated automatically. For example, if you change the score of one student in a test, the average that you used the function will automatically be recalculated. Furthermore, the chart will be updated to reflect the change.

A spreadsheet program is available as a stand-alone program (e.g., Microsoft Excel™ or Lotus 1-2-3™) or as part of integrated software, such as AppleWorks™ or MicrosoftWorks™. Once you have learned how to use a spreadsheet with any of these programs, you should be able to apply your knowledge to other spreadsheet programs.

Spreadsheets in Teaching and Learning

Spreadsheet is used in the classroom at all levels of education, whether it is for simple calculation and converting data into a chart, or for more serious data analysis. The primary applications of spreadsheet are to deal with numerical data such as keeping track of data, data analysis, and "what-if" problem solving. A few examples of how students can use a spreadsheet are as follows:

- Keeping track of data
  - Students can plant seeds in three pots, then place them in different locations—sunny outdoor, sunny window sill, and shady outdoor—and record the growth of the plants.
  - Students can record the temperature of five cities for a week, and report the findings by comparing the average temperature.
  - Students can track stocks and calculate profit or loss for a given investment.
  - Students can report the results of their fund-raising activity.

- Data analysis
  - Students can conduct a survey on their peers' opinions about an issue using a questionnaire of 10 questions rated on a scale from 1 to 5 (1 = strongly disagree, 5 = strongly agree), and summarize the results in averages and convert the data into charts.
  - Students can collect data on how many hours their classmates are using the computer per day for studying and playing, and find out the average for boys and girls.
  - Students can measure the hardness of water in water fountains and record it.

- Problem solving—"What-if" questions
  - Students can use a spreadsheet for calculating arithmetic functions when working on a logical-thinking problem. A sample question could be to project the future population in their town based on the last 5 years' population growth rate.

Teachers can use the spreadsheet for instructional activities with the students' participation as indicated in the preceding examples. Also, teachers can use the spreadsheet for instructional material development and for classroom management:

- Teaching the concepts
  - Teachers can teach different types of charts.
  - Teachers can teach the concept of percentage and interest.

- Keeping track of students' information
  - Teachers can keep track of students' scores and attendance. Some schools have adopted gradebook programs to keep the students' scores and attendance. In that case, teachers simply enter the students' names and scores. When teachers create their own gradebook with a spreadsheet program, they can design it as they wish but it requires more knowledge in using the program.
  - Teachers can keep track of students' performance—project checklist, assignment checklist, and so on.

- Planning and keeping the records
  - Teachers can plan and keep budget records.
  - Teachers can plan and keep supplies records.

 ## Overview of This Chapter

Activities and Projects

There are three activities to discuss spreadsheet features. After each activity a project is provided to apply what was covered in the activity.

Applications, Integration with Other Programs, and Summary

At the end of the chapter, the Applications section can be used for brainstorming and developing ideas to use spreadsheet in teaching and learning. Integration with Other Programs and Summary sections follow.

Icons to Watch

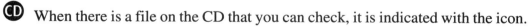 There are only minor differences between the Windows and Macintosh versions of Excel™. When a different instruction is required, it is indicated by the corresponding icons.

When there is a file on the CD that you can check, it is indicated with the icon.

More Information

How to use Excel™ as a database will be discussed in Chapter 6 "Database Techniques Using Excel."

Activity 1 : Working with Spreadsheets

This activity is based on the following scenario to create a spreadsheet:

"The students in a class are participating in a fund-raising activity by selling candles, cards, and candies. The class is divided into six (6) groups. There is one spreadsheet file that all six groups should use to report their results."

In Activity 1, the data from three groups will be shown.

This activity will guide you through the following tasks:

- Creating a spreadsheet document
- Understanding spreadsheet
- Entering data manually
- Entering data with AutoFill function
- Using mathematical formula to calculate total
- Using function to calculate sum (or total)
- Understanding types of data
- Creating a chart
- Adding a header or footer
- Printing a spreadsheet
- Working with the print range

 Creating a Spreadsheet Document

1. Open **Excel**™.

Microsoft Excel

2. Open **Excel Workbook** from the Project Gallery

Excel Workbook

1. Open **Excel**™.

Understanding Spreadsheets

When a spreadsheet document is created, the grids of rows and columns will appear. **Rows** run horizontally and are indicated by numbers. **Columns** run vertically and are indicated by letters. The intersection of a row and a column is a **cell**. The **active cell** (current cell) has a heavy border. The active cell indicates the location of the cursor. It is possible to select more than one cell, but only one cell is the active cell. The Active Cell Address indicates the location of the active cell where the cursor is located. In spreadsheet, the data are entered in the **Entry Bar**. The data in the Entry Bar will be placed in the active cell.

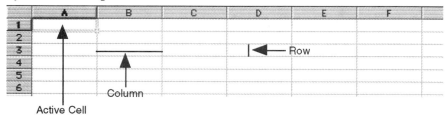

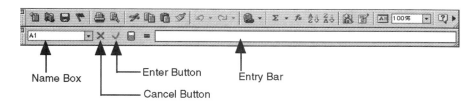

> **NOTE** If you don't see the toolbars, make sure to check **View** menu:
> View menu → **Formula Bar**,
> View menu → **Toolbars** → **Standard**, and
> View menu → **Toolbars** → **Formatting**.

Also, Excel™ allows the use of more than one sheet within one spreadsheet document. Multiple sheets are useful when you keep similar information. For example, you can keep information from different classes for the same semester—one class per sheet. Multiple sheets can also be useful when data are complicated, so that a segment of data can be stored in one sheet. The Sheet numbers are indicated in the bottom of the window. Excel™ uses the term "Workbook" to indicate a spreadsheet document.

\Sheet1 / Sheet2 / Sheet3 /

Entering Data Manually

To enter data, first locate the cursor in the cell by
- clicking the cell, or
- pressing the arrow key from the keyboard to move the cursor to the cell.

The cell becomes the **active cell**. Then, type in the data. The result will be shown in the **Entry Bar**. If it is correct, click the **Enter** button or press the Return (Macintosh) or Enter (Windows) key. Then, the data will be placed in the cell. If the entry is not correct, click the **Cancel** button or press the Delete (Macintosh) Backspace (Windows) key.

Enter data in the cells as follows:

	A	B	C	D	E
1	Group	Candles	Cards	Candies	Total
2		50	50	60	
3		45	70	70	
4		55	55	60	
5					

 Entering Data with AutoFill Function

AutoFill function allows filling in the repetitive data automatically. The types of data are days of the week, months of the year, or sequential data—for example, Group 1, Group 2, and so on.

	A	B
1	Monday	
2	Tuesday	
3	Wednesday	
4	Thursday	
5	Friday	
6	Saturday	
7	Sunday	

	A	B
1	Group 1	
2	Group 2	
3	Group 3	
4	Group 4	
5	Group 5	
6	Group 6	
7	Group 7	

Let's fill in Groups 1, 2, and 3 in Column Group with the AutoFill function.

1. Enter `Group 1` in Cell A2.

2. Click the right bottom corner of Cell A2.

	A	B	C	D	E
1	Group	Candles	Cards	Candies	Total
2	Group 1	50	50	60	
3		45	70	70	
4		55	55	60	
5					

Click the corner.

The AutoFill indicator will be shown.

3. Hold the mouse and drag it down to Cell A4.
   Group 2 and Group 3 will be filled automatically.

	A	B	C	D	E
1	Group	Candles	Cards	Candies	Total
2	Group 1	50	50	60	
3	Group 2	45	70	70	
4	Group 3	55	55	60	
5					

AutoFilled information

Using a Mathematical Formula to Calculate Total

The spreadsheet can calculate mathematical formula such as $+ - / *$. Let's calculate Cell E2. The formula is not case sensitive. B2 is the same as b2.

1. Get the mathematical formula to calculate the total of three cells—B2, C2, and D2. It should be B2+C2+D2. To make Excel™ understand this formula, it needs an equal sign (=) in front of the formula. So, it should be **=B2+C2+D2**.

2. Make Cell **E2** active as shown in the following figure.

	A	B	C	D	E
1	Group	Candles	Cards	Candies	Total
2	Group 1	50	50	60	
3	Group 2	45	70	70	
4	Group 3	55	55	60	
5					

Cell E2

3. Type the formula in the cell: =B2+C2+D2.

4. Click Enter button from the Formula Bar, or press Return/Enter.
   Cell E2 will have the total calculated. The result should be 160.

NOTE   You can use the mathematical symbols ($+ - / *$) for a complex calculation in math or science. For example, if you consider 20% for the value of Cell A1, 30% for B1, and 50% for C1, the formula would be =((A1*0.2)+(B1*0.3)+(C1*0.5)).

Using a Function to Calculate Sum (or Total)

In the previous section, you calculated the total by entering the mathematical formula. When there are only three cells to calculate, this method works well. But if there are more cells to calculate, it is more efficient to use the spreadsheet function.

There are three ways of entering the function to calculate sum (total) in the cell:
   a. Using **Function. . .** from the **Insert** menu.
   b. Typing the function directly.
   c. Using **AutoSum**.

Let's delete the current formula in Cell E2 so that you can try different methods.

1. Click Cell E2.
2. Press Delete (Macintosh) or Backspace (Windows).

You will calculate sum (total) in the column Total for Groups 1, 2, and 3 by using different methods.

Method 1: Using Function. . . from the Insert menu

Let's calculate Total in Cell E2 by using Function. . . from the Insert menu.

1. Make Cell **E2** active (click Cell E2).

2. Choose **Function. . .** from the **Insert** menu.
   The dialog box appears:

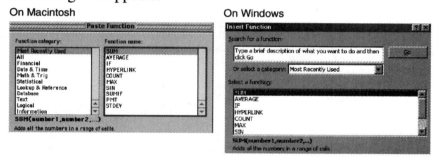

On Macintosh   On Windows

Some functions are classified in the category **Most Recently Used**. If you don't see the function that you are looking for, choose "All" from the **Function category** (Macintosh) or **Select a category** (Windows).

> **NOTE**   To get the function, instead of using the menu bar, you can also use the **Paste Function** (Macintosh) / **Insert Function** (Windows) from the Standard Toolbar (Macintosh) or the Formula bar (Windows).

fx Paste Function   *fx* Insert Function
      on Macintosh   on Windows

3. Select **SUM** from the Function Name box.

4. Click **OK**.
   The dialog box shows the possible cell addresses, and the formula is entered in the Entry Bar.

B2:D2 indicates "from Cell B2 to Cell D2," which are the values for Candles, Cards, and Candies for Group 1. The formula is not case sensitive. B2:D2 is the same as b2:d2.

5. Click **OK** from the formula dialog box.
   Cell E2 will have the total calculated.

	A	B	C	D	E
1	Group	Candles	Cards	Candies	Total
2	Group 1	50	50	60	160
3	Group 2	45	70	70	
4	Group 3	55	55	60	
5					

The cell has the calculated result.

NOTE   If the following dialog box appears, check **Don't ask me this again**, and click **NO**.

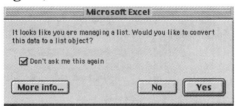

NOTE   In this example, the suggested cell addresses in the dialog box are correct. In case the cell addresses are not correct, you have to enter the correct cell addresses. It can happen when you don't include all the cells to calculate total, for example, calculating only Cells B2 and C2, or B2 and D2. If you calculate the total of Cells B2 and C2, the formula should be =SUM(B2:C2) or =SUM(B2+C2) or =B2+C2. If you calculate the total of Cells B2 and D2, the formula should be =SUM(B2+D2) or =B2+D2. B2 and D2 are not consecutive cells; therefore, the addresses should be indicated separately.

Method 2: Typing in the formula

Let's calculate Total in Cell E3 by typing in the formula directly.

When you know the spreadsheet formula, you can type in the formula directly in the cell, instead of going through the menu options. What are the cell addresses to be included for calculating total (sum)? They should be Group 2's Candles, Cards, and Candies. Therefore, the addresses are B3, C3, and D3. It is summarized as **B3:D3**. Don't type anything in the cell, yet!

1. Make Cell **E3** active.

2. What would be the correct function for Cell E3?
   It should be **=SUM(B3:D3)**. Type it in Cell E3.
   Don't forget the equal sign (=). The equal sign indicates that the entry is a function (formula), so that the computer is ready to calculate the result.

> **NOTE** To enter the cell address in the formula, instead of typing in the address, you can also click the first cell—in this case B3. Then, drag the mouse until the last cell—in this case D3. The addresses will be filled.

3. Click Enter button from the Entry Bar, or press Return/Enter.

Method 3: Using AutoSum

Let's calculate Total in Cell E4 by using AutoSum.

This method uses the **AutoSum** button from the toolbar.

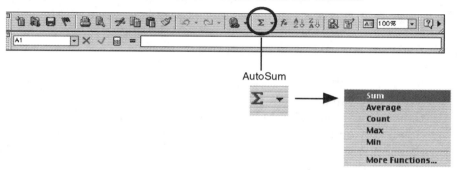

1. To use AutoSum, it is necessary to select (1) all the cells that are to be calculated and (2) the cell for the total—as the last cell. In this case, (1) cells **B4**, **C4**, **D4**, and (2) **E4** should be selected as follows:

	A	B	C	D	E
1	Group	Candles	Cards	Candies	Total
2	Group 1	50	50	60	160
3	Group 2	45	70	70	185
4	Group 3	55	55	60	
5					

Select the appropriate cells.

2. From the toolbar choose **AutoSum → Sum**.

> **NOTE** You have used three different methods for calculating sum (total) using the spreadsheet function. All methods yield the same result. You can choose any of these methods. The only thing that you have to be careful of when using AutoSum is the location of the cells. All the related cells should be next to each other. When the function (formula) is used, whether it is a mathematical formula or spreadsheet formula, data revision is much easier. For example, when you change the value for the entry (i.e., changing Group 1's Candles' value from 50 to 100), the Total will be calculated automatically.

Understanding Types of Data

You have just completed entering data in the spreadsheet.

	A	B	C	D	E
1	Group	Candles	Cards	Candies	Total
2	Group 1	50	50	60	160
3	Group 2	45	70	70	185
4	Group 3	55	55	60	170
5					

There are three types of data: **text** (or **label**), **value** (or **number**), and **function** (or **formula**). **Text** data contain characters. **Value** has only numbers. **Function** appears like a number in the cell, but it contains a formula to calculate the value data.

Let's find types of data from the spreadsheet.

- Click any cell in your spreadsheet that has **text** data. What you see in the cell is the same as what you see in the Entry Bar. How many cells have label data? There should be 8 cells: **A1**, **B1**, **C1**, **D1**, **E1**, **A2**, **A3**, and **A4**.
- Click any cell in your spreadsheet that has **value** data. What you see in the cell is the same as what you see in the Entry Bar. How many cells have number data? There should be 9 cells: **B2–D4**.
- What about Cells E2–E4? Click one of the cells. What you see in the cell is NOT the same as what you see in the Entry Bar. (If they are the same, you did not enter the function properly in the cell.) The cell contains the calculated result of the function. Cells **E2–E4** contain function data. Did you notice the equal sign (=) in the function? That equal sign indicates the entry is a function. Click Cell E2. E2 has a function: =**SUM(B2:D2)**. Change it to **SUM(B2:D2)**. It does not have the equal sign. Press Return/Enter. What kind of data is this? It is a text! *Make sure to put the function back in Cell E2, with the equal sign!*

 Creating a Chart

The spreadsheet data can be converted into a chart.

Let's convert **Group**, **Candles**, **Cards**, and **Candies** into a chart:

1. Select cells from A1 to D4.
   Why cells from A1 to D4? Because those cells have the data (Group, Candles, Cards, and Candies) that should be in the chart.

	A	B	C	D	E
1	Group	Candles	Cards	Candies	Total
2	Group 1	50	50	60	160
3	Group 2	45	70	70	185
4	Group 3	55	55	60	170
5					

2. Choose **Chart. . .** from the **Insert** menu.
   The chart dialog box appears.

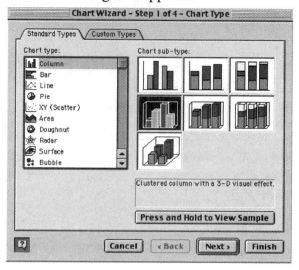

3. Let's select a style.
   3-1. For now, select the highlighted style in the preceding figure.
   3-2. Click **Next**.
       The following screen appears.

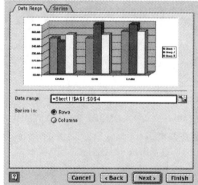

   3-3. Let's not make any change in this screen. Click **Next**.
       The following screen appears.

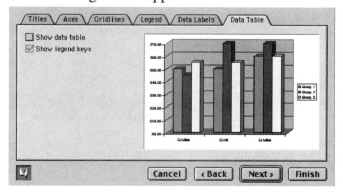

4. Let's add a title to the chart.

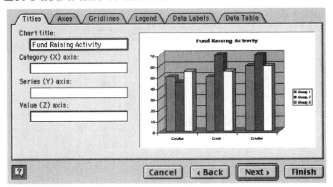

4-1. Choose **Titles** Tab.

4-2. In the Chart Title box, type `Fund Raising Activity`.

5. Let's work on the legend.
   The **legend** in the chart is the list of explained items of the chart.

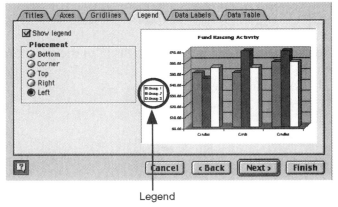

Legend

In your screen, the legend may appear in the right side.

5-1. Choose the **Legend** tab.

5-2. Choose a placement style—Bottom, Corner, Top, **Right, and Left.**
     In this example, Left is used.

5-3. Click **Next**.

6. Select the place of chart—**As object in** Sheet1.

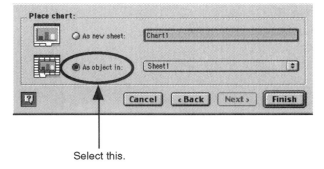

Select this.

7. Click **Finish**.

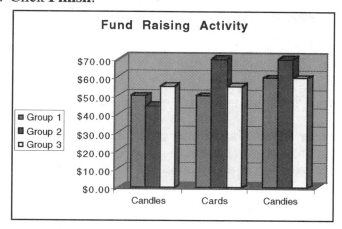

Roll over (and/or click) the mouse in different parts of the chart. The explanation of the chart will appear.

A chart is a drawing object. It is like an object in Drawing. When the dots appear around four corners of the chart, the chart is selected. The chart can be copied and pasted into other files, such as Word™ or PowerPoint™.

- To unselect the chart, click anywhere outside of the chart. The dots will disappear.
- To select the chart (near the boundary), click inside the chart. The dots will appear.

 Adding a Header or Footer

As in Word™ you can insert a header or footer in the Excel™ document. The process is similar.

Let's add **your name**, **class name**, **class time**, and **page number** in the header:

1. Choose **Header and Footer. . .** from the **View** menu.
   The dialog box appears. Both header and footer will be entered from here.

2. Select the **Header/Footer** tab.

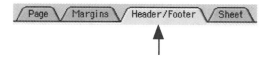

3. Let's select the type of the header.
   There are two general types of headers (and footers)—predesigned and customized. Predesigned headers come in various types but you cannot modify the contents. See the predesigned header options.

On the other hand, the customized header can be selected by clicking the button **Custom Header. . . .**

For this activity, choose **Custom Header. . .** because you need to type in the information that is not part of the predesigned list.

4. Enter **your name**, **class name**, **class time**, and **page number**.
   You can choose any section(s)—Left, Center, or Right. You can also enter some information in one section and some in another section. In this example, Left and Right sections are used.

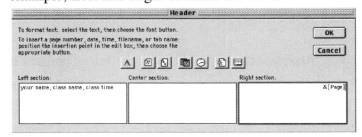

5. Click **OK**. Click **OK** again.

In the spreadsheet you may not see the header that you added. To see the header, choose **Print Preview** from the **File** menu. Make sure not to select the chart when using print preview. When finished, click **Close**.

➔ Printing a Spreadsheet

The spreadsheet in Excel™ can be printed page by page like a word processing document.

Let's print page 1 of the document.

1. To see the appearance of the page, choose **Print Preview** from the **File** menu. When finished, click **Close**.

2. Choose **Print** from the **File** menu.

3. Define the printing area.

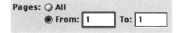

4. Click **Print/OK**.

Working with the Print Range

Print range is the area of the spreadsheet to be printed. Instead of printing page by page, you can select the area to be printed.

1. Let's set the print range.
    - 1-1. Select the cells that you want to print. Let's select Cells A1–E3. This is the data for Groups 1 and 2 only, not Group 3.
    - 1-2. From the **File** menu, choose **Print Area** → **Set Print Area**. The area is highlighted.

	A	B	C	D	E
1	Group	Candles	Cards	Candies	Total
2	Group 1	50	50	60	160
3	Group 2	45	70	70	185
4	Group 3	55	55	60	170
5					

   - 1-3. Choose **Print Preview** from the **File** menu.
     Note that Group 3 data are not included. Neither is the chart.
   - 1-4. Click **Close** to close the Print Preview.

2. Let's clear the print range.
    - 2-1. From the **File** menu, choose **Print Area** → **Clear Print Area**.

Finishing Touches

Save the document as SPREADSHEET1.

Project 1

In this project you will create a spreadsheet document and enter students' scores.

1. Create a new Excel™ document.
2. Enter the students' scores as follows.

	A	B	C	D	E	F	G
1	Student	Test 1	Test 2	Test 3	Test 4	Test 5	Total
2	S 1	77	78	80	82	84	
3	S 2	80	82	85	84	82	
4							

3. Calculate the total of 5 tests in Cells G2 and G3 by using the formula.
4. Create a chart for Statement and Test 1–Test 5. The chart should have a proper legend.
5. Add a header to show your name.
6. Print Preview to see the appearance of the spreadsheet.
7. Set the Print Range from Cells A1–F3.
8. Save the document as **SS1**.

> **CD** To see a finished sample project, check out the file **SS-Proj1** from the CD. (**Chapter 4** folder → **Projects** folder → **SS-Proj1**)

Activity 2 : Using Spreadsheet Features I

This activity is a continuation of Activity 1 to learn more about the essential features of the spreadsheet program.

File needed for this activity: SPREADSHEET1

This activity will guide you through the following tasks:

- Deleting a chart
- Using Fill Right
- Using Fill Down
- Selecting columns and rows
- Sorting data
- Changing text style
- Changing column width
- Changing row height
- Formatting the number (currency)
- Formatting cells: Alignment
- Adding a comment to the cell

Before You Begin

Open SPREADSHEET1.

 ### Deleting a Chart

A chart can be deleted. Let's delete the chart:

1. Select the chart, if it is not selected.

2. Press **Delete** (Macintosh) or **Backspace** (Windows).
   OR
   From the **Edit** menu choose **Clear** → **All**.

Using Fill Right

In Activity 1, you entered three groups' data. Now you will add the other three groups' data, as indicated below. Before you enter the data, take a close look. Each group has the same value for each entry.

Group	Candles	Cards	Candies	Total
Group 4	65	65	65	
Group 5	70	70	70	
Group 6	75	75	75	

When entering the same data, you can use a shortcut to enter the data without repeated typing. When the same data are in **horizontal** direction (in the row), use the **Fill Right** feature.

Let's use Fill Right to enter the data for Group 4.

1. Begin with Group 4. Enter **Group 4** in Cell A5; **65** in B5.

	A	B	C	D	E
1	Group	Candles	Cards	Candies	Total
2	Group 1	50	50	60	160
3	Group 2	45	70	70	185
4	Group 3	55	55	60	170
5	Group 4	65			
6					

2. Let's review the Fill Right feature.
   To enter Group 4's value for Cards and Candies, click Cell **B5**, and drag the mouse to Cell **D5**, as shown in the following figure. Why begin with B5? Because B5 has the data; C5 and D5 need the same data as B5.

	A	B	C	D	E
1	Group	Candles	Cards	Candies	Total
2	Group 1	50	50	60	160
3	Group 2	45	70	70	185
4	Group 3	55	55	60	170
5	Group 4	65			
6					

Select appropriate cells

3. From the **Edit** menu choose **Fill → Right**.
   Cells C5 and D5 will be filled with 65.

   In this example, there are only two cells to fill. If there are 50 cells to fill, it definitely saves time by using the Fill Right feature.

Let's use Fill Right to enter the data for Groups 5 and 6. The same steps are required as when entering data for Group 4. The difference is entering more than one set of data.

1. Enter Group names, Group 5 and Group 6 with AutoFill.

	A	B	C	D	E
1	Group	Candles	Cards	Candies	Total
2	Group 1	50	50	60	160
3	Group 2	45	70	70	185
4	Group 3	55	55	60	170
5	Group 4	65	65	65	
6	Group 5				
7	Group 6				
8					

2. Enter data in Cells B6 and B7.

	A	B	C	D	E
1	Group	Candles	Cards	Candies	Total
2	Group 1	50	50	60	160
3	Group 2	45	70	70	185
4	Group 3	55	55	60	170
5	Group 4	65	65	65	
6	Group 5	70			
7	Group 6	75			
8					

3. Select the cells to enter data with Fill Right function.

	A	B	C	D	E
1	Group	Candles	Cards	Candies	Total
2	Group 1	50	50	60	160
3	Group 2	45	70	70	185
4	Group 3	55	55	60	170
5	Group 4	65	65	65	
6	Group 5	70			
7	Group 6	75			
8					

Select the cells

4. From the **Edit** menu choose **Fill → Right**.
   Cells C6–D7 will be filled.

Using Fill Down

Fill Down is the same concept as Fill Right. The only difference is the direction. Fill Down enters the same data **vertically** in the columns.

Let's calculate Total for Groups 4, 5, and 6.

1. Click cell **E4**, and drag the mouse down to cell **E7**.
   Why E4 to E7? Remember that E4 has a function to calculate sum (total).
   When you fill down, the function will be filled down and the cell
   addresses in the function are adjusted for each cell.

	A	B	C	D	E
1	Group	Candles	Cards	Candies	Total
2	Group 1	50	50	60	160
3	Group 2	45	70	70	185
4	Group 3	55	55	60	170
5	Group 4	65	65	65	
6	Group 5	70	70	70	
7	Group 6	75	75	75	
8					

2. From the **Edit** menu choose **Fill → Down**.
   Cells E5–E7 will be filled.
   Therefore, when you calculate total, get the function (formula) in the first
   cell, and then fill down the rest of the cells.

Selecting Columns and Rows

Clicking the column address, A, B, C, . . . will select the whole column. Try it.

Clicking the row address, 1, 2, 3, . . . will select the whole row. Try it.

Sorting Data

Sorting data is rearranging the data according to alphabetical order or numerical order, in ascending or descending order. In Excel™ the sorting process has been simplified by selecting the necessary cells automatically. Before, it was up to the user to remember to select the cells. The sorting functions are available from the **Data** menu → **Sort. . .** or from the Standard Toolbar.

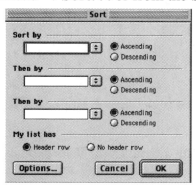

Standard Toolbar

Let's sort the data in **descending order of Total** (to have the highest total listed first) by using the **Data** menu → **Sort. . . .**

1. Click any cell that has data.

2. Choose **Sort. . .** from the **Data** menu.
   The Sort dialog box appears. At the same time the corresponding spreadsheet cells are selected.

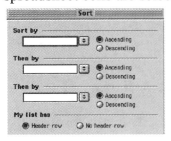
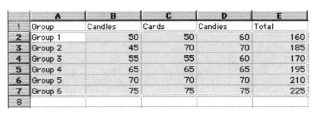

3. From the Sort dialog box, choose **Total** and **Descending**, as in the following figure:

4. Click **OK**.
   The spreadsheet is arranged in a new order.

	A	B	C	D	E
1	Group	Candles	Cards	Candies	Total
2	Group 6	75	75	75	225
3	Group 5	70	70	70	210
4	Group 4	65	65	65	195
5	Group 2	45	70	70	185
6	Group 3	55	55	60	170
7	Group 1	50	50	60	160
8					

Choose **Undo Sort** from the **Edit** menu, so that you can re-sort the data by using the other method.

Let's sort the data in **descending order of Total** (to have the highest total listed first) by using the Standard Toolbar.

1. Click a cell in the column Total. (It is not any cell. It should be one of the cells for sorting criteria—in this case, the cells for Total.)
   It could be any cell between E1 and E7.

2. Click Descending button from the Standard Toolbar.

 Descending

The spreadsheet is arranged in a new order.

What is the difference between these two sorting methods? If you sort data with only one criteria as you just did, it does not make any difference. However, if the data should be sorted in multiple levels, you should use the **Data** menu → **Sort. . .** option. Here is an example. You can sort the data by last name and then first name. The last names will be sorted and within the same last name the first names will be sorted. When there are the same last names, the second criteria—first name—will be applied.

 ## Changing Text Style

In the spreadsheet program, different styles and sizes of text are available as they were in the word processing program. The default style is plain text.

Let's change the text style of the column Total to boldface:

1. From the **View** menu, select **Toolbars** → **Formatting** to show the Formatting toolbar.

2. Select column **E** as follows, by clicking the column address E.

	A	B	C	D	E
1	Group	Candles	Cards	Candies	Total
2	Group 6	75	75	75	225
3	Group 5	70	70	70	210
4	Group 4	65	65	65	195
5	Group 2	45	70	70	185
6	Group 3	55	55	60	170
7	Group 1	50	50	60	160
8					

3. Choose Bold icon from the Formatting toolbar.

 ## Changing Column Width

Default column width in Excel™ is 8.43 on Windows and 10 on Macintosh. The higher the number, the wider the column. The column width can be adjusted by defining the column width from the **Format** menu → **Column** → **Width**. Also, the column width can be adjusted manually by dragging the column.

Let's make the width of columns **B–D** narrower by defining the column width (7).

1. Select Columns **B–D**.

	A	B	C	D	E
1	Group	Candles	Cards	Candies	**Total**
2	Group 6	75	75	75	**225**
3	Group 5	70	70	70	**210**
4	Group 4	65	65	65	**195**
5	Group 2	45	70	70	**185**
6	Group 3	55	55	60	**170**
7	Group 1	50	50	60	**160**
8					

2. From the **Format** menu, choose **Column** → **Width**.

3. In the Column Width dialog box, type in **7**.

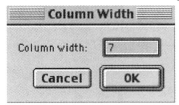

4. Click **OK**.
   Are the columns narrower?

Let's adjust the size of Column A manually.

1. Bring the cursor to the line between Columns A and B.
   The cursor will change its shape.

	A	B	C	D	E
1	Group	Candles	Cards	Candies	Total

2. Click the mouse and drag it the direction that you want to go.

	A	B	C	D	E
1	Group	Candles	Cards	Candies	Total
2	Group 6	75	75	75	225
3	Group 5	70	70	70	210

3. Release the mouse when the size of the column is adjusted.

There is no difference between the two methods for changing the column width. However, if you need to adjust more than one column, defining the column width is more practical.

 ## Changing Row Height

Default row height in Excel™ is 12.75 on Windows and 13 on Macintosh. The higher the number, the taller the row. As in the column width, the row height can be adjusted by defining the row height from the **Format** menu → **Row** → **Height**, or by dragging the row manually.

Let's make the height of Row 1 taller by defining the row height (20).

1. Select Row **1**.

	A	B	C	D	E
1	Group	Candles	Cards	Candies	Total
2	Group 6	75	75	75	225
3	Group 5	70	70	70	210
4	Group 4	65	65	65	195
5	Group 2	45	70	70	185
6	Group 3	55	55	60	170
7	Group 1	50	50	60	160
8					

2. From the **Format** menu, choose **Row → Height**.
3. In the Row Height dialog box, type in **20**.

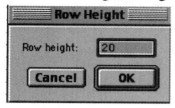

4. Click **OK**.
   Is the row taller?

NOTE   If you want to adjust the row height manually, do the same way as with the column width. The only difference is the direction—it should be vertical.

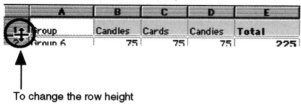

To change the row height

⮕ Formatting the Number (Currency)

In the current spreadsheet, the cells with values and functions indicate dollar amounts (e.g., dollar amount of candle sales). It is possible to change the format of the number in various ways. With the current spreadsheet, the currency—showing the dollar sign—would be the most appropriate format.

The number formatting function can be accessed from the Formatting Toolbar or from the **Format** menu → **Cells** → **Number** tab. Also, on Macintosh, the Formatting Palette can be used. The default number type is General.

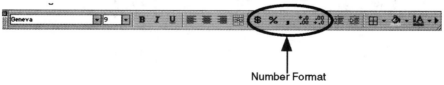

Number Format

Format menu → **Cells**

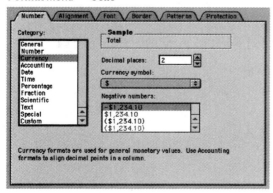

Formatting Palette (Macintosh only)

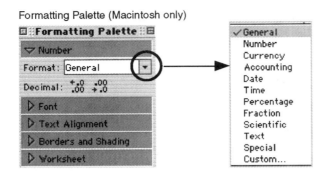

Let's change the format of all the number and function data to the **currency** format.

1. Select the cells that contain number and function data (Cells B2–E7).

	A	B	C	D	E
1	Group	Candles	Cards	Candies	Total
2	Group 6	75	75	75	225
3	Group 5	70	70	70	210
4	Group 4	65	65	65	195
5	Group 2	45	70	70	185
6	Group 3	55	55	60	170
7	Group 1	50	50	60	160
8					

2. Choose the **currency** format from
   * **Format** menu → **Cells** → **Number** tab,
   * Formatting Toolbar, or
   * Formatting Palette.

The data appear with the dollar sign.

	A	B	C	D	E
1	Group	Candles	Cards	Candies	Total
2	Group 6	$75.00	$75.00	$75.00	$225.00
3	Group 5	$70.00	$70.00	$70.00	$210.00
4	Group 4	$65.00	$65.00	$65.00	$195.00
5	Group 2	$45.00	$70.00	$70.00	$185.00
6	Group 3	$55.00	$55.00	$60.00	$170.00
7	Group 1	$50.00	$50.00	$60.00	$160.00
8					

 ## Formatting Cells: Alignment

The contents of the cells can be aligned as in word processing. Let's align the Cells B1–E1 to Centered alignment:

1. Select Cells **B1–E1**.

2. Choose the Centered alignment from the Formatting Toolbar.

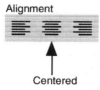

Alignment

Centered

Adding a Comment to the Cell

Adding a **comment** to the cell is to keep a note for you. It does not affect the spreadsheet function such as calculation or sorting. To add a comment, use **Comment** from the **Insert** menu.

Let's add a comment in Cell A1 to indicate the groups were sorted in descending order of Total.

1. Click Cell **A1**.

2. Choose **Comment** from the **Insert** menu.
   The dialog box appears:

3. Type the comment: The groups are sorted in descending order of Total.

4. To hide the comment, from the **View** menu, uncheck **Comments**.
   The dialog box disappears, and the indication of comment is shown in the cell.

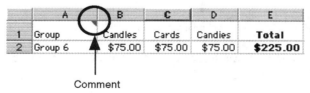

Comment

NOTE   To delete the comment:
   1. Select the cell that has the comment to be deleted.
   2. From the **Edit** menu choose **Clear → Comments**.

Finishing Touches

1. Create a bar chart to indicate **Group**, **Candles**, **Cards**, and **Candies** information.
   • Do not include total in the chart.
   • Show the Group list.

- Add the title of the chart.
- Show the legend.

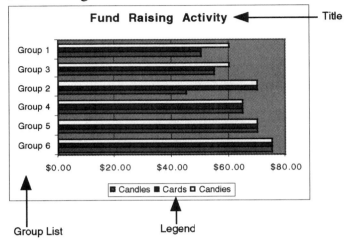

If your chart is missing elements, see the following information:

- Did you get the chart without proper information?

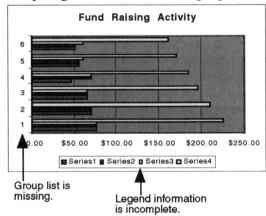

Then, you did not select the appropriate cells. Delete the chart, select the appropriate cells, and create a new chart.

- Did you get a blank chart?

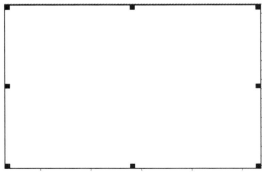

Then, you did not select the cells to convert the data into a chart. Select the appropriate cells before creating a chart.

2. Save the document as SPREADSHEET2.

This is a continuing project from Project 1 to add more spreadsheet features.

1. Open **SS1**.
2. Save the file as **SS2**.
3. Delete the chart.
4. Clear the defined Print Range.
5. Enter data for Cells A4–A11 and B4–F8 as in the following figure. (Use AutoFill for Cells A4–A8. Use Fill Right for Cells B4–F8.)

	A	B	C	D	E	F	G
1	Student	Test 1	Test 2	Test 3	Test 4	Test 5	Total
2	S 1	77	78	80	82	84	401
3	S 2	80	82	85	84	82	413
4	S 3	80	80	80	80	80	
5	S 4	95	95	95	95	95	
6	S 5	92	92	92	92	92	
7	S 6	88	88	88	88	88	
8	S 7	76	76	76	76	76	
9	Average						
10	Highest						
11	Lowest						

6. Calculate the total scores in Cells G4–G8 by using Fill Down.
7. Sort the data in descending order of Total.
8. Make the column width of Columns B–F smaller.
9. Make the row height of Row 1 taller.
10. Make text style in Row 1 bold.
11. Add comments to at least one cell.
12. Create a bar chart for Student and Test 1–Test 5.
    The chart should show Students S1–S7 and Test 1–Test 5.
13. Format Cells B1–G1 as centered alignment.
14. Save the file.

> **CD** To see a finished sample project, check out the file **SS-Proj2** from the CD. (**Chapter 4** folder → **Projects** folder → **SS-Proj2**)

Activity 3: Using Spreadsheet Features II

In Activities 1 and 2, the most used spreadsheet features were covered. In Activity 3, we will review what was discussed earlier and we will acquire several new spreadsheet features.

A new spreadsheet will be created to compare the temperature among cities.

This activity will guide you through the following tasks:

- Formatting the number (date)
- Inserting or deleting a column
- Inserting or deleting a row
- Calculating average
- Finding the maximum value
- Finding the minimum value
- Formatting the number (decimal precision)
- Understanding Relative Reference and Absolute Reference
- Using Lookup function
- Formatting cells: Merging cells
- Formatting cells: Borders and shading

Before You Begin

1. Create a new Excel™ document.

2. Enter data as in the following figure. These are weather data to record the daily high temperatures in several Midwestern cities in the United States, between November 14 and 17.

   Just type the data. You may notice that the dates—11/14, 11/15, . . .—do not appear as you type. Instead, you may see 14-Nov, 15-Nov. . . .

	A	B	C	D	E	F
1	City	11/14	11/15	11/16	11/17	Average
2	Chicago, IL	41	41	42	36	
3	Minneapolis, MN	33	33	28	27	
4	Madison, WI	39	35	36	30	
5	Indianapolis, IN	39	40	43	36	
6	Average					
7	Warmest					
8	Coldest					
9						

3. Adjust Column A size big enough to show the text.
   (See Activity 2 → Changing Column Width.)

4. Save the file as SPREADSHEET3.
   Save the file often during the activity.

 ## Formatting the Number (Date)

In Activity 2, changing the format of number to Currency was discussed. Let's explore one more option of the number format. It is the **date**. Formatting the date can be accessed from the **Format** menu → **Cells** → **Number** tab.

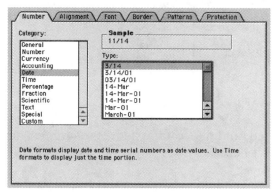

Let's change the date format.

1. Select Cells **B1–E1** that have dates.
2. From the **Format** menu, choose **Cells** → **Number** tab.
3. Select **Date** from the Category.
4. Select the Type as in the preceding figure.
5. Click **OK**.

The date format in Cells B1–E1 has been changed.

	A	B	C	D	E	F
1	City	11/14	11/15	11/16	11/17	Average
2	Chicago, IL	41	41	42	36	
3	Minneapolis, MN	33	33	28	27	
4	Madison, WI	39	35	36	30	
5	Indianapolis, IN	39	40	43	36	
6						

Date format changed

Inserting or Deleting a Column

In spreadsheet when more columns are needed, they can be inserted.

Let's insert a column to add the temperature data of November 13 between columns A and B.

1. Select Column **B**.

	A	B	C	D	E	F
1	City	11/14	11/15	11/16	11/17	Average
2	Chicago, IL	41	41	42	36	
3	Minneapolis, MN	33	33	28	27	
4	Madison, WI	39	35	36	30	
5	Indianapolis, IN	39	40	43	36	
6	Average					
7	Warmest					
8	Coldest					
9						

2. Choose **Columns** from the **Insert** menu.

	A	B	C	D	E	F	G
1	City		11/14	11/15	11/16	11/17	Average
2	Chicago, IL		41	41	42	36	
3	Minneapolis, MN		33	33	28	27	
4	Madison, WI		39	35	36	30	
5	Indianapolis, IN		39	40	43	36	
6	Average						
7	Warmest						
8	Coldest						
9							

A new column is inserted, and the column addresses are rearranged. Adjust Column B size, if necessary.

3. Enter the data in Column B, the newly inserted column. And then change the date format in Cell B1, as in the following figure:

	A	B	C	D	E	F	G
1	City	11/13	11/14	11/15	11/16	11/17	Average
2	Chicago, IL	36	41	41	42	36	
3	Minneapolis, MN	35	33	33	28	27	
4	Madison, WI	33	39	35	36	30	
5	Indianapolis, IN	40	39	40	43	36	
6	Average						
7	Warmest						
8	Coldest						
9							

(You may not see the highlights in the column.)

If the following dialog box appears, check **Don't ask me this again**, and click **NO**.

NOTE   To delete a column:
1. Select the column to be deleted.
2. Choose **Delete** from the **Edit** menu.

Inserting or Deleting a Row

Inserting a row is adding an extra row in between existing ones. It is the same as inserting a column.

Let's insert a row between Rows 5 and 6. When finished it should be as in the following figure:

	A	B	C	D	E	F	G
1	City	11/13	11/14	11/15	11/16	11/17	Average
2	Chicago, IL	36	41	41	42	36	
3	Minneapolis, MN	35	33	33	28	27	
4	Madison, WI	33	39	35	36	30	
5	Indianapolis, IN	40	39	40	43	36	
6							
7	Average						
8	Warmest						
9	Coldest						
10							

1. Select Row 6—`Average`.
2. Choose **Rows** from the **Insert** menu.

NOTE   To delete a row:
1. Select the row to be deleted.
2. Choose **Delete** from the **Edit** menu.

 ## Calculating the Average

In Activity 1, how to calculate sum (total) was discussed. There are three methods to use the function for calculating sum. How to calculate average is the same. There are also three methods to use the function for calculating average:

   a. Using **Function. . .** from the **Insert** menu.
      This is the same as using the **Insert Function** from the Formula Bar on Windows and the **Paste Function** from the Standard Toolbar on Macintosh.

   b. Typing the function directly.
   c. Using **AutoAverage** in the toolbar.

You will calculate average in Cells G2–G4 by using three different methods.

Let's calculate average of daily temperature between 11/13–11/17 in Cell G2 by using Function. . . from the Insert menu.

1. Make Cell **G2** active (Select Cell **G2**).

2. Choose **Function. . .** from the **Insert** menu.

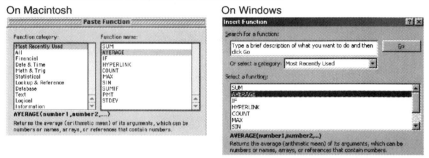

   If you don't see the function that you are looking for, choose "All" from the **Function category** (Macintosh) or **Select a category** (Windows).

3. Select **AVERAGE** from the Function Name box.

4. Click **OK**.
   The dialog box shows the possible cell addresses, and the function is entered in the Entry Bar.

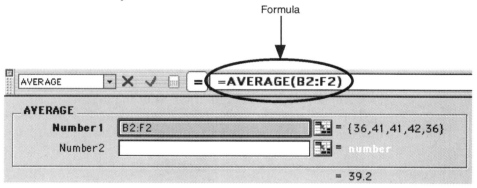

   B2:F2 indicates "from Cell B2 to Cell F2," which are the values for Chicago's temperature between 11/13–11/17.

5. Click **OK** from the formula dialog box.
   Cell G2 will have the total calculated.

	A	B	C	D	E	F	G
1	City	11/13	11/14	11/15	11/16	11/17	Average
2	Chicago, IL	36	41	41	42	36	39.2
3	Minneapolis, MN	35	33	33	28	27	
4	Madison, WI	33	39	35	36	30	
5	Indianapolis, IN	40	39	40	43	36	
6							

The cell has the calculated result.

NOTE   In this example, the suggested cell addresses are correct. In case the cell addresses are not correct, you have to enter the correct cell addresses. It can happen when you don't include all the cells to calculate average, for example, calculating only Cells B2 and C2, or B2 and D2. If you calculate the average of Cells B2 and C2, the formula should be =AVERAGE(B2:C2) or =AVERAGE(B2+C2). If you calculate the average of Cells B2 and D2, the formula should be =AVERAGE(B2+D2). B2 and D2 are not consecutive cells; therefore, the addresses should be indicated separately.

Let's calculate average in Cell G3 by typing the formula directly.

When you know the formula, you can type in the formula directly instead of going through the menu options. What are the cell addresses for which we are calculating average? They should be Minneapolis's temperature between 11/13–11/17. Therefore, the addresses are B3, C3, D3, E3, and F3. It is summarized as **B3:F3**. Don't type anything in the cell, yet!

1. Make Cell **G3** active. (Select Cell G3.)

2. What would be the correct function for Cell G3?
   It should be =**AVERAGE(B3:F3)**. Type it in Cell G3.
   Don't forget the equal sign (=). The equal sign indicates that the entry is a function (formula), so that the computer is ready to calculate the result.

   NOTE   To enter the cell address in the formula, instead of typing in the address, you can click the first cell—in this case, B3. Then, drag the mouse until the last cell—in this case, F3. The addresses will be filled.

3. Click the Enter button from the toolbar, or press Return/Enter.

Let's calculate total in Cell G4 by using AutoAverage.

This method uses the **AutoAverage** button from the toolbar.

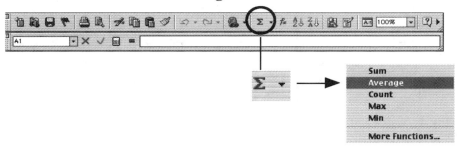

1. To use AutoAverage, it is necessary to select (1) all the cells that are to be calculated and (2) the cell for the total—as the last cell. In this case, (1) Cells **B4**, **C4**, **D4**, **E4**, **F4** and (2) **G4** should be selected as follows:

	A	B	C	D	E	F	G
1	City	11/13	11/14	11/15	11/16	11/17	Average
2	Chicago, IL	36	41	41	42	36	39.2
3	Minneapolis, MN	35	33	33	28	27	31.2
4	Madison, WI	33	39	35	36	30	
5	Indianapolis, IN	40	39	40	43	36	
6							

Select the appropriate cells.

2. From the toolbar, choose **AutoSum** → **Average**.

NOTE You have used three different methods for average. All methods yield the same result. You can choose any of these methods. The only thing that you have to be careful of when using AutoAverage is the location of the cells. All the related cells should be next to each other.

Calculate average in Cell G5. Fill Down would be the easiest.

	A	B	C	D	E	F	G
1	City	11/13	11/14	11/15	11/16	11/17	Average
2	Chicago, IL	36	41	41	42	36	39.2
3	Minneapolis, MN	35	33	33	28	27	31.2
4	Madison, WI	33	39	35	36	30	34.6
5	Indianapolis, IN	40	39	40	43	36	39.6
6							

(You may not see the same highlights in the cells.)

Calculate average in Cells B7–G7.

This is to calculate the average temperature of each day. How to calculate average in a row is the same as in a column. Just make sure to get the right cell addresses for calculation. The easiest way is to calculate average in Cell B7, and then Fill Right the rest. The result is shown in the following figure:

	A	B	C	D	E	F	G
1	City	11/13	11/14	11/15	11/16	11/17	Average
2	Chicago, IL	36	41	41	42	36	39.2
3	Minneapolis, MN	35	33	33	28	27	31.2
4	Madison, WI	33	39	35	36	30	34.6
5	Indianapolis, IN	40	39	40	43	36	39.6
6							
7	Average	36	38	37.25	37.25	32.25	36.15
8	Warmest						
9	Coldest						
10							

(You may not see the same highlights in the cells.)

On Windows, you may get the error message. This message appears because the cells in Row 6 were not included for calculating average and Excel™ assumes that the cells were not included accidentally.

Error Message

If so, click the error message and choose **Ignore Error**.

Finding the Maximum Value

By now you know how to calculate sum (total) and average. There are more useful functions in the spreadsheet. One of them is finding the maximum value. Maximum value is the largest value in the data set. For example, in the current spreadsheet what would be the warmest temperature for each day?

As in calculating sum or average, there are three ways to find the maximum value:

a. Using **Function. . .** from the **Insert** menu.
   This is the same as using the **Insert Function** from the Formula Bar on Windows and the **Paste Function** from the Standard Toolbar on Macintosh.

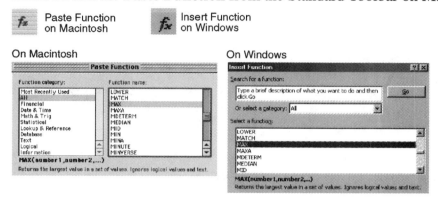

Be careful with the cell addresses. For example, Cell B8 should calculate the highest value among Cells B2–B5.

b. Typing the formula directly.
   =**MAX(cell address:cell address)**
      This formula is when the cells are consecutive. In this activity, Cell B8 should have =**MAX(B2:B5)**.
   =**MAX(cell address, cell address, cell address, . . .)**
      This formula is when the cells are not consecutive.

c. Using **AutoMax** from the toolbar.

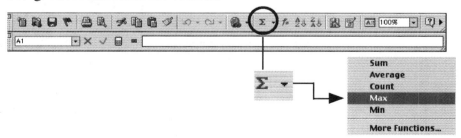

Be careful with the cell addresses.
Cell B8 should have =MAX(B2:B5).

Find the warmest temperature for each day in Cells B8–G8:

> The easiest way is to find the maximum value in Cell B8 (the warmest temperature on 11/13 among cities). And then Fill Right the rest of the cells. When finished, it should be as in the following figure:

	A	B	C	D	E	F	G
1	City	11/13	11/14	11/15	11/16	11/17	Average
2	Chicago, IL	36	41	41	42	36	39.2
3	Minneapolis, MN	35	33	33	28	27	31.2
4	Madison, WI	33	39	35	36	30	34.6
5	Indianapolis, IN	40	39	40	43	36	39.6
6							
7	Average	36	38	37.25	37.25	32.25	36.15
8	Warmest	40	41	41	43	36	39.6
9	Coldest						
10							

 ## Finding the Minimum Value

You have just used the function to find the maximum value. The opposite of the function is to find the minimum value. Minimum value is the smallest value in a set of data. For example, in the current spreadsheet, what would be the coldest temperature for each day?

The procedure to find the minimum value is exactly the same as finding the maximum value, except the function to use. The function to find the minimum value is =**MIN**.

> a. Using **Function. . .** from the **Insert** menu.
> This is the same as using the **Insert Function** from the Formula Bar on Windows and the **Paste Function** from the Standard Toolbar on Macintosh.

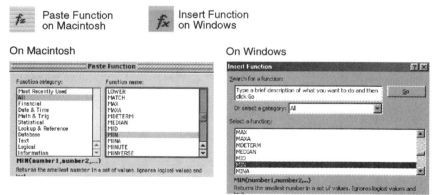

> Be careful with the cell addresses. For example, Cell B9 should calculate the lowest value among the Cells B2–B5.

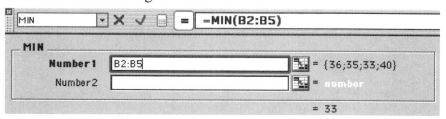

b. Typing the function directly.
=MIN(cell address:cell address)
This formula is when the cells are consecutive. In this activity, Cell B9 should have **=MIN(B2:B5)**.
=MIN(cell address, cell address, cell address, . . .)
This formula is when the cells are not consecutive.

c. Using **AutoMin** from the toolbar.
Be careful with the cell addresses.

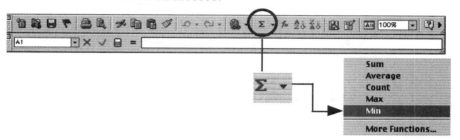

Find the coldest temperature for each day in Cells B9–G9:

The easiest way is to find the minimum value in Cell B9 (the coldest temperature on 11/13 among cities). And then Fill Right the rest of the cells. When finished, it should be as in the following figure:

	A	B	C	D	E	F	G
1	City	11/13	11/14	11/15	11/16	11/17	Average
2	Chicago, IL	36	41	41	42	36	39.2
3	Minneapolis, MN	35	33	33	28	27	31.2
4	Madison, WI	33	39	35	36	30	34.6
5	Indianapolis, IN	40	39	40	43	36	39.6
6							
7	Average	36	38	37.25	37.25	32.25	36.15
8	Warmest	40	41	41	43	36	39.6
9	Coldest	33	33	33	28	27	31.2
10							

Formatting the Number (Decimal Precision)

So far we have used Currency and Date formats. Let's explore one more option of the number format. It is the **decimal precision**. The decimal precision indicates the digits below the decimal point. The decimal precision is controlled from the **Format** menu → **Cells** → **Number** tab.

Look at the current spreadsheet. There are three styles of the decimal precision: zero, one, and two digits below the decimal point. The value data that we entered do not have digits below the decimal point (B2–F5). The averages have different digits below the decimal point—different decimal precisions.

Let's unify the format of average values to have one-digit decimal precision. That means the values will have one digit below the decimal point as a fixed style.

1. Let's begin with column G. Select Column **G**.

2. From the **Format** menu, choose **Cells** → **Number** tab.

3. Choose **Number** from the Category.

4. Change it to one-digit decimal precision, as in the following figure:

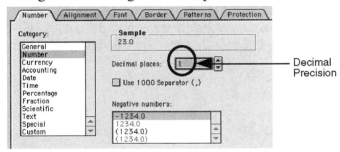

5. Click OK.
   The decimal precision has been changed to one digit:

	A	B	C	D	E	F	G
1	City	11/13	11/14	11/15	11/16	11/17	Average
2	Chicago, IL	36	41	41	42	36	39.2
3	Minneapolis, MN	35	33	33	28	27	31.2
4	Madison, WI	33	39	35	36	30	34.6
5	Indianapolis, IN	40	39	40	43	36	39.6
6							
7	Average	36	38	37.25	37.25	32.25	36.2
8	Warmest	40	41	41	43	36	39.6
9	Coldest	33	33	33	28	27	31.2
10							

6. Change the decimal precision of Row 7—Average—to one digit.

	A	B	C	D	E	F	G
1	City	11/13	11/14	11/15	11/16	11/17	Average
2	Chicago, IL	36	41	41	42	36	39.2
3	Minneapolis, MN	35	33	33	28	27	31.2
4	Madison, WI	33	39	35	36	30	34.6
5	Indianapolis, IN	40	39	40	43	36	39.6
6							
7	Average	36.0	38.0	37.3	37.3	32.3	36.2
8	Warmest	40	41	41	43	36	39.6
9	Coldest	33	33	33	28	27	31.2
10							

➔ Understanding Relative Reference and Absolute Reference

When you fill down or fill right the functions, the cell's value reference is changing relatively based on the cell. For example, Cell **B9** has the function, =**MIN(B2:B5)**. When this function is filled right, the next cell, **C9**, has the function =**MIN(C2:C5)**. The cell changed its reference—relevant cell address. This is called the **Relative Reference**.

The relative reference is applied to the functions that you used, =**SUM**, =**AVERAGE**, =**MAX**, and =**MIN**. So far, we have used only the relative reference.

The **Absolute Reference** is the opposite concept of the relevant reference. The cell does not change its reference. Therefore, the reference is absolute regardless of which cell is being calculated. We will explore the absolute reference in the following section—Using Lookup Function.

Using the Lookup Function

Lookup is an advanced function in spreadsheet that assigns the value automatically based on the preset ranges—**compare range** and **result range**. A good example is setting up a gradebook to enter the grade automatically—A for 90%, B for 80%, and so forth.

In the current spreadsheet, you will insert a comment on the weather for each city based on its average temperature. If the average temperature is 30.0 and above and below 32.0, the comment would be "Cold." The lowest value of the range is 30.0. In this example, the lowest possible temperature is 30.0 and the highest is 50.0. The **compare range** is titled as Range; the **result range** is Comment in the following figure.

Range (Compare Range)	Comment (Result Range)
30.0	Cold
32.0	Chilly
39.5	Mild
50.0	Mild

For example, if the temperature is 34 degrees, it will be matched up to the compare range, and then the result will be given—"Chilly" because any temperature from 32.0 degrees to less than 39.5 degrees is defined as "chilly."

1. Let's create the **compare range** and the **result range**.
   The compare range and the result range will be created in the same spreadsheet. In empty cells define the compare range and the result range—in this example, Cells **K1–L5**. Type the following data in Cells **K1–L5**.

K	L
Range	Comment
30	Cold
32	Chilly
39.5	Mild
50	Mild

2. Type Comment in Cell H1.
   Column H will have the appropriate comment according to the temperature and the defined range.

	A	B	C	D	E	F	G	H
1	City	11/13	11/14	11/15	11/16	11/17	Average	Comment
2	Chicago, IL	36	41	41	42	36	39.2	
3	Minneapolis, MN	35	33	33	28	27	31.2	
4	Madison, WI	33	39	35	36	30	34.6	
5	Indianapolis, IN	40	39	40	43	36	39.6	
6								
7	Average	36.0	38.0	37.3	37.3	32.3	36.2	
8	Warmest	40	41	41	43	36	39.6	
9	Coldest	33	33	33	28	27	31.2	
10								

3. Insert function LOOKUP.

   3-1. Activate Cell H2.

   3-2. Insert the function **LOOKUP**.

        Use Insert menu → Functions. . . , or use Paste Function / Insert Function from the Standard Toolbar / Formula Bar.

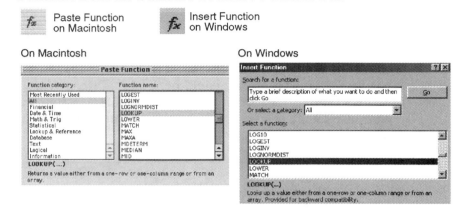

   3-3. Click **OK**.

   3-4. Select the **argument**.

        In this activity, it should be **Lookup_Value**, **Array**. **Lookup value** is what we want to compare. In this activity, it is the average temperature of each city. **Array** is the compare range and the result range for the Lookup function. In this example, it has two columns—Columns K and L.

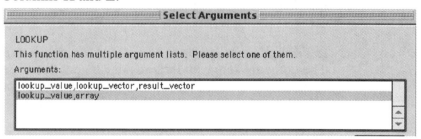

   3-5. Click **OK**.

        The LOOKUP dialog box appears:

4. Enter information in the LOOKUP dialog box.

   4-1. Before entering the information, move the dialog box so that you can see the cells that you are working on. Move the dialog box by dragging its top part.

	A	B	C	D	E	F	G	H
1	City	11/13	11/14	11/15	11/16	11/17	Average	Comment
2	Chicago, IL	36	41	41	42	36	39.2	=LOOKUP()
3	Minneapolis, MN	35	33	33	28	27	31.2	
4	Madison, WI	33	39	35	36	30	34.6	
5	Indianapolis, IN	40	39	40	43	36	39.6	
6								
7	Av							
8	Wa							
9	Col							
10								
11								
12								

LOOKUP
Lookup_value [ ] = any
Array [ ] = reference
=

   4-2. Enter the **Lookup value**.

In this example, the Lookup value is the average temperature. Therefore, the Lookup value for Cell **H2** is Cell **G2**. While **Lookup_value** box is selected, click Cell **G2** (or type in G2).

LOOKUP
Lookup_value [G2] = 39.2
Array [ ] = reference
=

   4-3. Enter **Array**.

Array is the compare range and the result range for the Lookup function. In this activity, these are the cells K2–L5. Enter **K2:L5** in the **Array** box.

LOOKUP
Lookup_value [G2] = 39.2
Array [K2:L5] = {30,"Cold";32,"Chi
= "Chilly"

   4-4. Click **OK**.

In Cell H2, the word "Chilly" will appear:

	A	B	C	D	E	F	G	H
1	City	11/13	11/14	11/15	11/16	11/17	Average	Comment
2	Chicago, IL	36	41	41	42	36	39.2	Chilly
3	Minneapolis, MN	35	33	33	28	27	31.2	
4	Madison, WI	33	39	35	36	30	34.6	
5	Indianapolis, IN	40	39	40	43	36	39.6	
6								

5. Let's examine the absolute value.

   5-1. First, Fill Down the function in Cells H3–H5.

	A	B	C	D	E	F	G	H
1	City	11/13	11/14	11/15	11/16	11/17	Average	Comment
2	Chicago, IL	36	41	41	42	36	39.2	Chilly
3	Minneapolis, MN	35	33	33	28	27	31.2	#N/A
4	Madison, WI	33	39	35	36	30	34.6	#N/A
5	Indianapolis, IN	40	39	40	43	36	39.6	#N/A
6								

Cells H3–H5 do not have the correct results. What went wrong?

5-2. Let's check the Lookup value and array.
Click Cell H2. Examine the Lookup value and array.

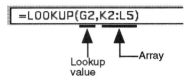

Click Cell H3. Examine the Lookup value and array.

```
=LOOKUP(G3,K3:L6)
```

In Cell H3, Lookup value G3 is correct because it is the temperature to be compared. What about the array? It indicates K3:L6. Is this correct? In this activity, the array was defined in Cells K2–L5. That should not be changed. In other words, *the compare range and the result range should not be changed!* They should be the **absolute reference**. Cells H2, H3, H4, and H5 should have the same compare range and the result range—the Array.

6. Let's make the array—the compare range and the result range—the **absolute reference**.
   6-1. Activate Cell H2.
   6-2. Type the dollar sign ($) for every part of the absolute reference, as follows:

   ```
   =LOOKUP(G2,$K$2:$L$5)
   ```

   6-3. Click Enter button from the toolbar, or press Return/Enter in the keyboard.

7. Fill Down the function in Cells H3–H5.

	A	B	C	D	E	F	G	H
1	City	11/13	11/14	11/15	11/16	11/17	Average	Comment
2	Chicago, IL	36	41	41	42	36	39.2	Chilly
3	Minneapolis, MN	35	33	33	28	27	31.2	Cold
4	Madison, WI	33	39	35	36	30	34.6	Chilly
5	Indianapolis, IN	40	39	40	43	36	39.6	Mild
6								

Check Cells H3–H5. The array value should be the same—$K$2:$L$5.

Formatting Cells: Merging Cells

Merging cells in spreadsheet is to combine the cells, in either vertical or horizontal direction. It is the same as formatting table cells in word processing.

Let's format Rows 1 and 2 as in the following figure:

	A	B	C	D	E	F	G	H
1				Dates				
2	City	11/13	11/14	11/15	11/16	11/17	Average	Comment
3	Chicago, IL	36	41	41	42	36	39.2	Chilly
4	Minneapolis, MN	35	33	33	28	27	31.2	Cold
5	Madison, WI	33	39	35	36	30	34.6	Chilly
6	Indianapolis, IN	40	39	40	43	36	39.6	Mild

1. Insert a Row as the first Row.
   (For instructions, see the previous section—Inserting or Deleting a Row.)

2. In Cell B1, type `Dates`.

3. Let's merge Cells B1–F1.

   3-1. Select Cells B1–F1.
   3-2. From the Formatting Palette, choose Text Alignment section, and then check **Merge Text**.

   The cells will be merged.
   3-3. Align the text `Dates` centered in the merged cell.

   3-1. Select Cells B1–F1.
   3-2. Choose **Merge and Center** from the Formatting toolbar.

   The cells are merged and the text is centered.

4. Merge the Cells A1–A2.
   Keep the Left alignment.

   On Windows, it automatically formats the merged cell as the Centered alignment. Click the Left alignment from the toolbar.

5. Merge the Cells G1–G2.
   Keep the Left alignment.

6. Merge the Cells H1–H2.

NOTE   As you inserted a row, the absolute reference cell addresses (for the array) for the Lookup function have been shifted from K2–L5 to K3–L6. Check Cells H3, H4, H5, and H6. Did you notice that the cell addresses for the array have been updated to K3–L6? Also, did you notice that the absolute reference was kept in Cells H3, H4, H5, and H6?

Formatting Cells: Borders and Shading

A **border** is a line or lines around the cell. **Shading** is filling in the cell with color and pattern. Borders and shading can be accessed from the **Format** menu → **Cells. . . .**

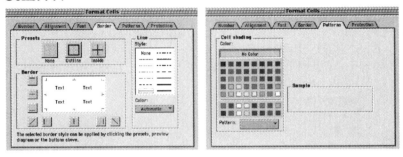

Let's format the cells with borders and shading as follows:

	A	B	C	D	E	F	G	H
1				Dates				
2	**City**	11/13	11/14	11/15	11/16	11/17	**Average**	**Comment**
3	Chicago, IL	36	41	41	42	36	39.2	Chilly
4	Minneapolis, MN	35	33	33	28	27	31.2	Cold
5	Madison, WI	33	39	35	36	30	34.6	Chilly
6	Indianapolis, IN	40	39	40	43	36	39.6	Mild
7								
8	Average	36.0	38.0	37.3	37.3	32.3	36.2	
9	Warmest	40	41	41	43	36	39.6	
10	Coldest	33	33	33	28	27	31.2	

1. Make the text bold as indicated in the preceding figure.

2. Let's add a double line as the border in the bottom of Row 2.
   2-1. Select the cells in Row 2.
   2-2. Choose **Cells. . .** from the **Format** menu.
   2-3. Choose the **Border** tab.

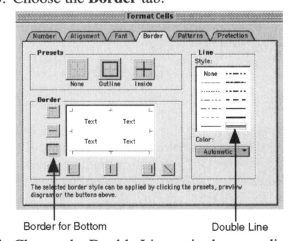

Border for Bottom   Double Line

   2-4. Choose the Double Line as in the preceding figure.
   2-5. Choose the Border for Bottom as in the preceding figure.
        (Always choose the line style first, then the border location.)
   2-6. Click **OK**.

3. Let's add shading to Cells A1–A10.
   3-1. Select Cells A1–A10.
   3-2. Choose **Cells. . .** from the **Format** menu.
   3-3. Choose the **Patterns** tab.

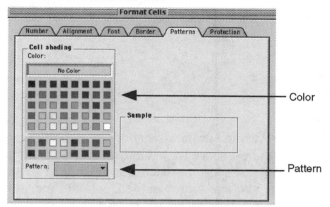

3-4. Choose color (and pattern).
3-5. Click **OK**.

4. Add shading to Cells B1–F2.

5. Add a thick line as a border to the right side of the cells in Column H.

6. Add a line as a border to the bottom of the cells in Row 7.

7. Add a thick line as a border to the bottom of the cells in Row 10.

8. Add a line as a border to the right side of the cells in Column A.

Finishing Touches

1. Make the text `City, Dates, Average, Comment` bold.
2. Save the file.

Project 3

This is a continuing project from Project 2 to add more spreadsheet features.

1. Open **SS2**.
2. Save the file as **SS3**.
3. Sort the data in ascending order of Column A—`Student`. Only S1-S7, not other cells. (Hint: Before sorting, you need to select Rows 2-8).

4. Add a row after Row 8.

	A	B	C	D	E	F	G	H	I
1	Student	Test 1	Test 2	Test 3	Test 4	Test 5	Total	Average	Grade
2	S 1	77	78	80	82	84	401		
3	S 2	80	82	85	84	82	413		
4	S 3	80	80	80	80	80	400		
5	S 4	95	95	95	95	95	475		
6	S 5	92	92	92	92	92	460		
7	S 6	88	88	88	88	88	440		
8	S 7	76	76	76	76	76	380		
9									
10	Average								
11	Highest								
12	Lowest								

5. Calculate Average in the row and in the column by using the function.
6. Find the highest score for each test in Row 11 by using the function.
7. Find the lowest score for each test in Row 12 by using the function.
8. Format the average scores in the Decimal Precision 1 digit.
9. Use the LOOKUP function to enter the grade as follows:
   The range is based on the average score. An A will be 90 points, a B will be 80 points, and so forth.

Range	Grade
0	F
60	D
70	C
80	B
90	A
100	A

10. Format the spreadsheet with borders and shading.
11. Save the file.

> **CD** To see a finished sample project, check out the file **SS-Proj3** from the CD. (**Chapter 4** folder → **Projects** folder → **SS-Proj3**)

Integration with Other Programs

The data in spreadsheet—the entered data or the chart—can be used in other application programs, such as word processing and presentation.

When the data in spreadsheet are copied and pasted in a Word™ document, the rows and columns are kept so that it seems like a table as in the following example:

Group	Candles	Cards	Candies	Total
Group 1	50	50	60	**160**
Group 3	55	55	60	**170**
Group 2	45	70	70	**185**

You can even modify the data in the cells, but the functions to calculate would not work. The cells with the functions keep only the calculated value, not the functions. Therefore, it would not recalculate the values automatically.

When the data in spreadsheet are copied and pasted in a word processing document other than a Word™ document, the rows and columns may not seem like a table, but other characteristics are the same as in a Word™ document.

When a chart in spreadsheet is copied and pasted in a word processing document, including a Word™ document, the chart is the same as a graphic.

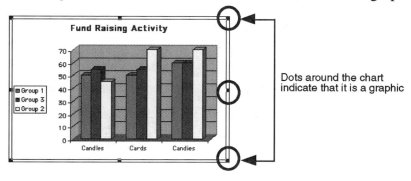

Dots around the chart indicate that it is a graphic

Also, the data and the chart in spreadsheet can be copied and pasted in a Power-Point™ document. In this case, both the data and the chart become a graphic. Therefore, the data cannot be modified.

Applications

In this chapter, the spreadsheet hands-on skills and the ideas for using spreadsheet in the classroom were discussed. Examine the possibilities of applying spreadsheet programs in education.

1. Collect ideas on how to use spreadsheet with the students. You can refer to the section *Getting Started* to create your own ideas. Consider the following example to get started:

Example

Activity Purpose: To project the future population in three towns based on the last 5 years' population growth rate.

Activity Description: Towns A, B, and C in Lake County have different population growth rates during the last 5 years. The current population and the growth rate over 5 years are in the following table.

	Current Population	Growth Rate
Town A	24,300	3%
Town B	23,600	5%
Town C	21,200	7%

What if the towns keep the same population growth rate for the next 10 years? Which town will have the largest population?

The spreadsheet can be constructed as follows:

	A	B	C	D
1			Population	
2		Current	5 yrs later	10 yrs later
3	Town A	24300	25029	25780
4	Town B	23600	24780	26019
5	Town C	21200	22684	24272

After 10 years, Town B will have the largest population.

How was it calculated? Since the population growth rate is reported for a 5-year period, it is easier to calculate the population after 5 years, and then after 10 years. Cells C3, C4, and C5 have the formulas to calculate the population after 5 years.

- Cell C3: =**B3*1.03**

   [The equal sign (=) indicates that it is a formula. Cell **B3** has the current population. * means to multiply. 3% is equal to 0.03. Adding 3% to the current status (1.0) is **1.03**.]

- Cell C4: =**B4*1.05**
- Cell C5: =**B5*1.07**

Once the population after 5 years is calculated, the population after 10 years can be calculated in Cells D3–D5 by filling right from Cells C3–C5 (Edit menu → Fill → Right). If you check Cells D3–D5, the following formulas will be shown:

- Cell D3: =**C3*1.03**
- Cell D4: =**C4*1.05**
- Cell D5: =**C5*1.07**

2. Collect ideas on how to use spreadsheet as a teacher for classroom management and teaching. You can refer to the section *Getting Started* to create your own ideas.

3. Create a lesson plan in which you can integrate the spreadsheet by expanding the ideas in the section *Getting Started* or by developing your own ideas. Include the following components:
   - Subject matter
   - Grade level
   - Purpose of the activity (lesson objective)
   - Target audience
     - Prior knowledge on the lesson objective (any related content covered?)
     - Computer skill
     - Any other information that you want to include
   - Environment
     - Location: In the classroom or in the lab?
     - Number of computers needed
   - Description of instructional activity
     - Description on how the lesson will proceed and how spreadsheet will be used

4. Collect ideas on how to integrate spreadsheet with other programs. You can refer to the section *Integration with Other Programs* to create your own ideas.

Summary

1. Spreadsheet programs are designed to manipulate numerical data.

2. There are various applications of the spreadsheet program in education for students and teachers.

3. From the hands-on activities, the following tasks were covered:
   - Data entry and process
     - Creating a spreadsheet document
     - Entering data manually and with AutoFill function
     - Understanding types of data
     - Inserting columns and rows
     - Creating and deleting a chart
     - Using Fill Right and Fill Down
     - Sorting data
   - Using functions to calculate
     - Calculating total
     - Calculating average
     - Finding the maximum value
     - Finding the minimum value
     - Understanding Relative Reference and Absolute Reference
     - Using Lookup function
   - Spreadsheet appearance
     - Changing column width and row height
     - Changing text style
     - Formatting the number—Currency, Date, Decimal precision
     - Formatting cells: Borders and shading
     - Adding a header
   - Notes and printing
     - Adding comments to cells
     - Printing a spreadsheet
     - Working with the print range

Chapter 5

Microsoft PowerPoint: The Presentation Tool

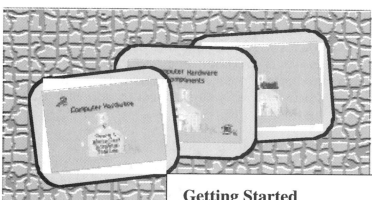

Getting Started
**Activity 1: Creating a Presentation
   with a Template**
   Project 1
**Activity 2: Creating a Presentation
   from Scratch**
   Project 2
Activity 3: Formatting Presentation I
   Project 3
Activity 4: Formatting Presentation II
   Project 4
Integration with Other Programs
Applications
Summary

Getting Started

 Features of Presentation Programs

Presentation programs are designed to develop computer-based presentation material, especially for a large group. It replaces the transparencies with an overhead projector as a visual aid; it also adds sound, animations, and movie clips to make multimedia presentations. Creating a presentation in Microsoft Office™ is done with PowerPoint™.

The features of presentation programs can be summarized as follows:

- **Slides**. A presentation program is composed of slides. A **slide** is a predetermined page that fits the entire computer screen when the presentation is viewed.

- **Slide layout**. The slide layout provides the design scheme of the slide. It has various styles and arrangements for heading, text, or graphic. Because a presentation is to show the information in front of a large group, the font size used is significantly larger than that normally used in a word processing file.

- **Template**. A **template** is a predesigned slide layout with background graphic and selected font style. It is very easy to create a presentation by using the template. Also, when you are proficient in using graphic programs and have an idea, you can create your own slide appearance as the slide master.

- **Slide components**. A slide can have text, graphic, sound, animations, and movie clips to deliver information.

- **Visual effects**. To present the information more dynamically, it is possible to add visual effects to the slide components and to the slide transition (for advancing to the next slide).

- **Links and non-linear navigation**. Most presentations are created linearly. They go from one slide to the next. However, by linking the slide components, you can also create a presentation with non-linear navigation. It doesn't just go to the next slide; it can be linked to any slide.

- **Saving as web page**. A presentation file can be converted into a web page.

PowerPoint™ is a popular presentation program. Besides PowerPoint™, as an easy-to-use authoring program, HyperStudio™ can also be used to create a presentation (although HyperStudio™ is not designed just for presentation). The Presentation in AppleWorks™ is also a simple presentation program.

 ## Presentation in Teaching and Learning

A presentation program can be viewed as a specialized graphic program for creating a presentation. Therefore, its application in teaching and learning is specifically related to the presentation. Both teachers and students can use the presentation program to create their presentations, even multimedia presentations. One thing to remember when creating a presentation is how to organize the information. Presentation is different from writing a paper with word processing. The presenter should get to the key point to capture the audience's attention—avoid lengthy text—and should fill in the detailed information.

The following are a few examples of how students can develop a presentation:

- Students can develop a presentation based on their research paper. For example, the students can plant seeds in three pots, then place them in different locations—sunny outdoor, sunny window sill, and shady outdoor—and record the growth of the plants. During the project, the students could take photos of the plants and keep the records of the growth in spreadsheet. In the presentation, the students can add the photos and the charts generated with a spreadsheet program.
- Students can create their interactive résumés with non-linear navigation. Adding photos—such as a photo of the student or photos of the student involved in activities—would be informative and stylish.
- Students can create a presentation on a book report to share the information with the class.

The following are a few examples of how teachers can develop a presentation:

- Teachers can develop a presentation for lecture.
- Teachers can develop a presentation for meetings with parents about students' activities.

 ## Overview of This Chapter

Activities and Projects

There are four activities that cover the presentation techniques. They begin with using a template and move to creating a presentation with one's own design and formatting the presentation. After each activity a project is provided to apply what was covered in the activity.

Applications, Integration with Other Programs, and Summary

At the end of the chapter, the Applications section can be used for brainstorming and developing ideas to use presentation tools in teaching and learning. Integration with Other Programs and Summary sections follow.

Icons to Watch

(WIN)   **(MAC)**   There are a few differences between the Windows and Macintosh versions of PowerPoint™. When a different instruction is required, it is indicated by the corresponding icons.

(CD)   When there is a file on the CD that you can check, it is indicated with the icon.

More Information

It is recommended to complete Chapter 3 "Graphic Tools and Page Design in Microsoft Office" before this chapter.

Activity 1: Creating a Presentation with a Template

In this activity a PowerPoint™ presentation will be developed by using a template.

"Students in Group 1 are developing a presentation about their paper—Computer Hardware."

This activity will guide you through the following tasks:

- Creating a PowerPoint™ document with a template
- Understanding the Slide Layout
- Working with text
- Viewing the toolbars
- Adding slides
- Browsing the slides
- Viewing the presentation

If you are familiar with the contents covered in this activity, you may skip the activity, but you may want to complete Project 1 at the end of the activity.

CD To browse the tasks that are covered in this activity by viewing a movie, check out the file **PR-win** (Windows) or **PR-mac** (Macintosh) from the CD. If this is the first time to use PowerPoint, it is strongly recommended. (**Chapter 5** folder → **MoreInfo** folder → **PR-win** or **PR-mac**)

➲ Creating a PowerPoint™ Document with a Template

Follow the instructions for Macintosh or Windows.

1. Open PowerPoint™.

Microsoft PowerPoint

2. From the Project Gallery window, choose **Presentations**, as in the following figure. (Click the triangle.)

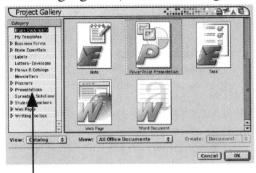

To choose a Template

NOTE   If you click PowerPoint Presentation, it will create a blank presentation. Because we will use a template in this activity, do not click this.

3. From the Presentations folder, choose **Designs**.

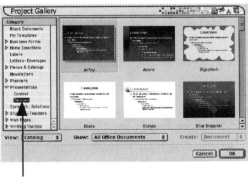

Choose Design Template

The design templates will be shown.

4. Browse the templates and choose one. In this example the template named Blends is selected. You can choose a different one.

1. Open PowerPoint™.

Powerpnt

2. From the Task Pane, choose **From Design Template**.

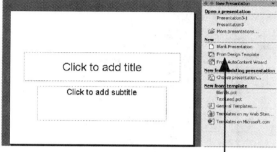

From Design Template

3. Browse the templates and choose one. In this example the template named Blends is selected. You can choose a different one.

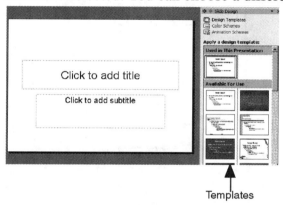

Templates

Understanding the Slide Layout

A **slide** is a defined space in the presentation. You can add slides as you need. Each time you add a new slide the New Slide window will appear. This is a list of slide layouts, such as having a title slide, title and text, title and two-column text, title and graphic, title and organization chart, title only, or blank. You can choose a style. Then it will create a style on top of the template that you chose. The slide layout is a suggested list. For example, it does not mean you have to choose the option with graphic in order to add a graphic. Graphic—clip arts or pictures—can be added on any slide layout.

The New Slide layout is shown:

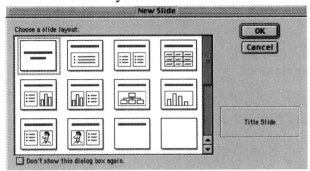

From the Task Pane, choose **Slide Layout**.

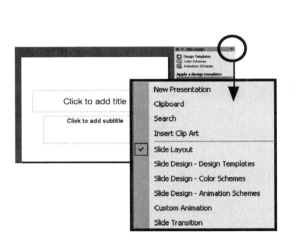

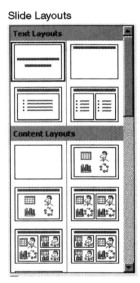

➲ Working with Text

Let's create the first slide—title slide.

1. From the Slide Layout, choose **Title Slide**.

    (It doesn't always have to be the Title Slide style for the title. It could be Title Only or even Blank.)

A blank slide will be created.

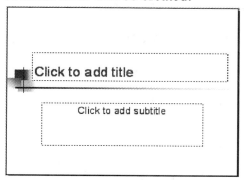

2. Type text in the text boxes as in the following figure.

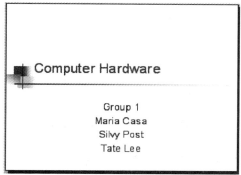

As you type, the slide information appears in the left column of the screen, as in the following figure. This gives a bird's-eye view of the slides.

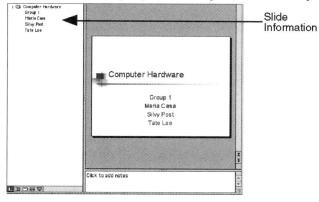

On Windows, if you don't see the slide information, choose the **Outline** tab.

Viewing the Toolbars

Let's show the toolbars that are used most often. These are Standard Toolbar, Formatting, and Drawing Toolbar.

- From the **View** menu, choose **Toolbars** → **Standard**
- From the **View** menu, choose **Toolbars** → **Formatting**
- From the **View** menu, choose **Toolbars** → **Drawing**

On Windows, if the toolbars are not shown in two rows, choose the option at the end of the toolbar and select **Show Buttons on Two Rows**.

Once the toolbars are set up, choose the **Toolbar Options** ( ) at the end of the Formatting Toolbar and select **Add or Remove Buttons**. Make sure that **Increase Paragraph Spacing** and **Decrease Paragraph Spacing** are selected.

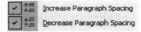

 Adding Slides

A new slide can be added from the **Insert** menu → **New Slide**. A new slide can also be added from the **Toolbar** → **New Slide**.

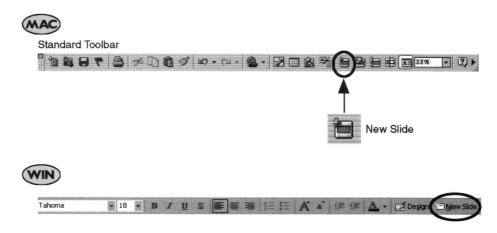

Let's add a new slide (for Slide #2) with the **Bulleted List / Title and Text** style.

1. Choose **New Slide. . .** from the **Insert** menu, or choose **New Slide** button from the toolbar.

2. Choose the **Bulleted List** (Macintosh) / **Title and Text** (Windows) style.

3. Type text as follows:

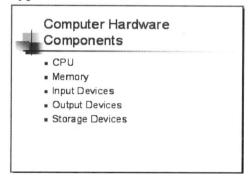

Add a new slide for Slide #3.

1. Add a new slide with the **Title Only** style.

2. Type text as follows:

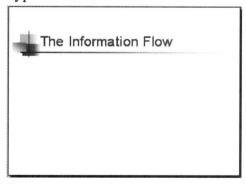

Add a new slide for Slide #4.

1. Add a new slide with the **Blank** style.

2. Add WordArt as in the following figure.
   WordArt is on the Drawing Toolbar. Use about 24-point text. Once the WordArt is inserted, you may have to stretch it to see the text better.

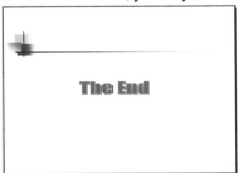

Browsing the Slides

To browse the slides that you created use one of the following ways:
   a. Clicking the slide number from the slide outline.
   b. Scrolling up and down with the scroll bar or the arrows.

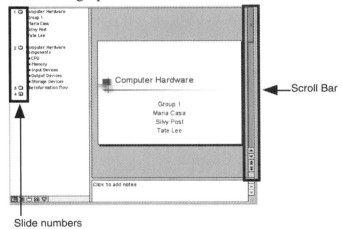

Slide numbers

Viewing the Presentation

Your presentation is roughly finished. Let's run the **slide show** to view the presentation. The slide show can be run in three ways:
   a. **Slide Show** menu → **View Show**
   b. **View** menu → **Slide Show**

c. From the Status Bar → **Slide Show** button, as in the following figure.

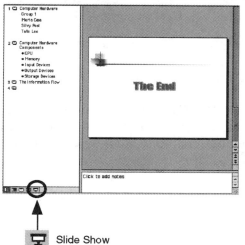

Slide Show

There is no difference between the first two methods that are using the menu bar. Both run the slide show from the first slide. But the last option, using the Status Bar → Slide Show button, runs the slide show from the current slide. For example, if you are in Slide 4, the slide show will begin from Slide 4. Therefore, if you want to see the entire presentation, choose the options from the menu (Slide Show menu → View Show, View menu → Slide Show). On the other hand, if you want to check the current slide and the subsequent ones, choose Status Bar → Slide Show button.

Let's view the presentation.

1. Run the slide show by using one of the three methods described above.

2. Use the following direction to navigate the slide show:
   - To advance to the next slide, click the mouse. After the last slide it automatically quits the slide show mode.
   - To stop the slide show before the last slide, press **esc** from the keyboard, or from the screen choose **End Show**.

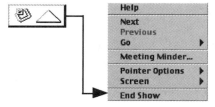

Finishing Touches

Save the file as PRESENTATION1.

Project 1

This project is to create a PowerPoint™ presentation with a template.

1. Create a presentation about the Food Guide Pyramid.
   * Use a template.
   * Create 3 or 4 slides. (It is OK not to include all the food groups. For the Food Guide Pyramid information, you can refer to the files that you finished in the previous chapters, **WP4**, **DR2**, and **DR3**.)
2. Save the file as **PR1**.

Activity 2: Creating a Presentation from Scratch

In this activity a PowerPoint™ presentation will be developed from scratch without using the template. The same contents of the slides will be created as in Activity 1. But this time, you will begin with a blank presentation and create your own slide master and background.

This activity will guide you through the following tasks:

- Creating a blank PowerPoint™ document
- Designing the Slide Master
- Designing the background

 Creating a Blank PowerPoint™ Document

Follow the instructions for Macintosh or Windows.

1. Open **PowerPoint**™.

2. From the Project Gallery, choose **PowerPoint Presentation**.

 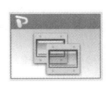

New Slide window appears:

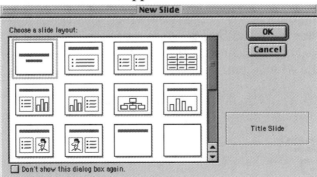

3. Choose **Title Slide**.

A blank slide appears.

1. Open **PowerPoint**™.

2. Choose **Blank Presentation** from the Task Pane.

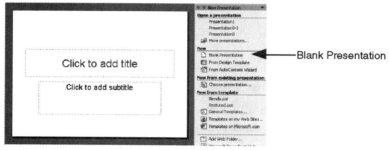

A blank slide is ready.

 ## Designing the Slide Master

The **slide master** contains common elements for every slide such as text style for the title, text style for the main text, graphics, and buttons.

In Activity 1, you used a template so that you didn't have to design your own slide master. In this activity, you will design the slide master first. Once the slide master is done, entering information in individual slides is exactly the same as using a template. Designing your own slide master can be useful especially if you have a background graphic or a logo to show in every slide. The slide master can be accessed from the **View** menu → **Master** → **Slide Master**.

Let's choose text style in the slide master. This defines the text style for the title and main text.

1. Have the Formatting Toolbar showing
   (View menu → Toolbars → Formatting).

2. From the **View** menu, choose **Master** → **Slide Master**.

   NOTE   If the warning message appears, click **OK**.

The slide master appears.

3. Select the **Master title style**, and choose text style—font, size, color, and style.

Text color in PowerPoint™ can be controlled from the Formatting Toolbar. There are differences in the color palettes available between Windows and Macintosh versions. See the following instructions.

When you choose **More Font Colors**, different color palettes appear—CMYK Picker, Crayon Picker, RGB Picker, and a few others. For a simple color picking, Crayon Picker would be the easiest. You can try different methods.

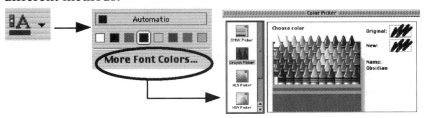

When you choose **More Colors**, you will see more color options.

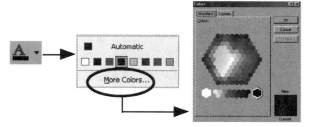

4. Select the **Master text styles**, and choose text style—font, size, color, and style.

You can choose different font and/or color, but don't make it more distinctive than the title.

5. Select the rest of the text styles—Second through Fifth levels; and choose text style—font, size, color, and style. The Fourth and Fifth levels are hardly used, but just format them for the slide master.

Let's add a graphic in the slide master. For this activity you will add a clip art or picture, change the size, and transform it to watermark/washout style.

1. While you are in the Slide Master, insert a clip art or picture.

2. Make the graphic—clip art or picture—bigger.

3. Transform the clip art to Watermark/Washout.
   Watermark/Washout makes the picture light. For the background, it is good to have a graphic not distracting the text on top.
   (If you need instructions to make the Watermark/Washout effect, see Chapter 3 "Graphic Tools and Page Design in Microsoft Office" → Activity 3 Formatting a Picture → Color Control.)

➲ Designing the Background

Background applies the fill-in background color to the slide master. The background can be accessed from the **Format** menu → **Background. . .** (or **Side Background**).

Let's add a background color, pattern, and/or texture.

1. While you are in the Slide Master, choose **Background. . .** (or **Slide Background**) from the **Format** menu.

   NOTE Background can be added in individual slides as well, not only to the Slide Master. When it is applied to the Slide Master, all the slides that share the slide master will have the background. If the background is applied while you are viewing an individual slide, you can apply the background only to the slide or to all the slides.

Background dialog box appears.

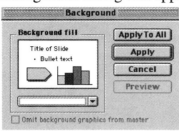

2. Fill in color, pattern, and/or texture.
   You can even insert a picture as a background. But for this activity, let's stay with the color, pattern, and/or texture. To fill color, pattern, and/or texture, use the following options.

Choose color, pattern, and/or texture that is a contrast to the text, so that the text can be more visible with the background.

3. Click **Apply**.

4. The Slide Master and the background are finished. Go back to Normal view (View menu → Normal).

Finishing Touches

1. Add slides as follows:

Slide #1

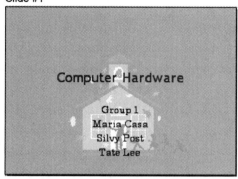

Slide #2

Slide #3

Slide #4

2. View the presentation.
3. Save the file as PRESENTATION2.

Project 2

This project is to create a PowerPoint™ presentation from scratch.

1. Create a presentation about the Food Guide Pyramid.
   - Design the Slide Master and Background.
   - Use the same or similar information from Project 1 (**PR1** file).
   - Create 3 or 4 slides. (It is OK not to include all the food groups.)
2. Save the file as **PR2**.

Activity 3: Formatting Presentation I

In this activity the PowerPoint™ presentation developed from Activity 2 will be formatted by adding graphics, animation, sounds, movies, and slide transition.

File needed for this activity: PRESENTATION2

This activity will guide you through the following tasks:

- Rearranging the slides
- Deleting a slide
- Formatting text: Paragraph spacing
- Formatting text: Indentation
- Formatting Text Placeholders
- Adding graphics: Clip arts and pictures
- Adding movies
- Adding sounds
- Adding animation
- Adding custom animation
- Adding slide transition

Before You Begin

1. Open the file PRESENTATION2.

2. Save the file as PRESENTATION3.
   Save the file often during the activity.

3. Add six more slides as follows:

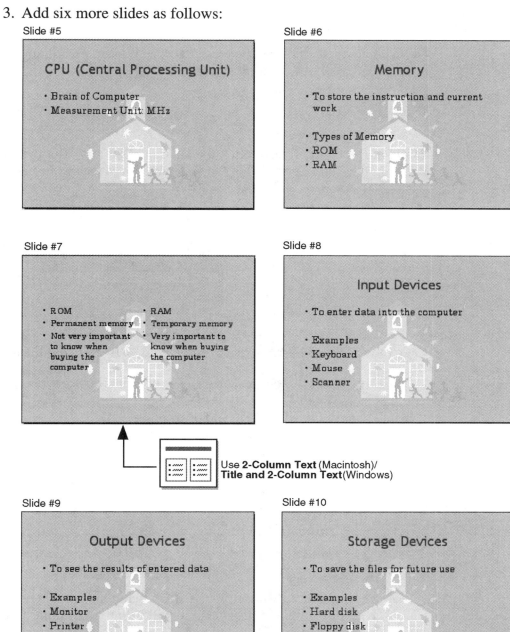

Slide #5

CPU (Central Processing Unit)

- Brain of Computer
- Measurement Unit: MHz

Slide #6

Memory

- To store the instruction and current work

- Types of Memory
- ROM
- RAM

Slide #7

- ROM
- Permanent memory
- Not very important to know when buying the computer

- RAM
- Temporary memory
- Very important to know when buying the computer

Slide #8

Input Devices

- To enter data into the computer

- Examples
- Keyboard
- Mouse
- Scanner

Use **2-Column Text** (Macintosh)/
Title and 2-Column Text (Windows)

Slide #9

Output Devices

- To see the results of entered data

- Examples
- Monitor
- Printer

Slide #10

Storage Devices

- To save the files for future use

- Examples
- Hard disk
- Floppy disk
- Zip disk
- Writable CD

4. View the slide show.

Rearranging the Slides

Occasionally, you may need to rearrange the slides in a different sequence. It can be done in **Normal** view or **Slide Sorter** in the **View** menu.

While in the Normal view, click the slide number and drag it to the new location. While in the Slide Sorter, click the slide and drag it to the new location.

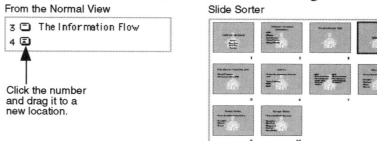

Let's move Slide #4—The End—after Slide #10 by using the slide sorter.

1. Choose **Slide Sorter** from the **View** menu.
2. Click Slide #4.
3. Drag it after Slide #10, and drop it.
   Now The End slide becomes Slide #10.
4. Double-click a slide to come back to Normal view, or choose Normal from the View menu.

Deleting a Slide

Slides can be deleted. Let's delete Slide #3—The Information Flow.

1. Be in Slide #3.
2. Choose **Delete Slide** from the **Edit** menu.
   The slide will be deleted. There will be a total of nine slides in the presentation.

Formatting Text: Paragraph Spacing

Paragraph spacing is to increase or decrease the spacing between lines. The increased paragraph spacing leaves more spaces between lines, and the decreased paragraph spacing creates dense lines. Paragraph spacing can be controlled from the Formatting Toolbar.

Paragraph Spacing

Let's decrease the paragraph spacing of the names in Slide #1.

1. Select the names.

2. Click **Decrease Paragraph Spacing** a couple of times.
   The names will be placed closer.

In the same slide—Slide #1— change the word Group 1 to a different color, so that it doesn't look like part of the names.

 ## Formatting Text: Indentation

Indentation is to promote or demote the text. Demoting leaves more indentation, while promoting deletes the indentation. Indentation can be controlled from the Formatting Toolbar.

Indentation

Let's demote the text (increase the indentation of the text) in Slide #4—Memory.

1. Select text to be demoted—**ROM** and **RAM**.
2. Click **Demote** (Macintosh)/**Increase Indent** (Windows) button.

Demote the text (increase the indentation of the text) in Slide #5–Slide #8 as follows:

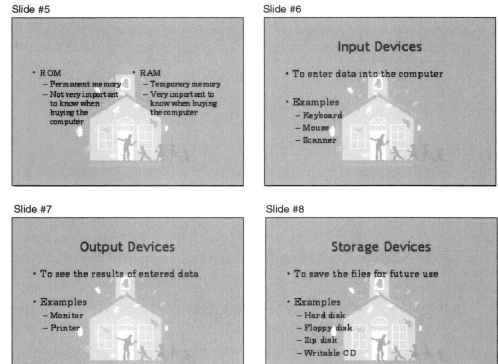

Formatting Text: Placeholders

Most slides in PowerPoint™ have predesigned text placeholders. It provides a uniformed appearance from one slide to the next. However, if you have to move or make the placeholder slightly bigger, you can modify it. For example, in the title page the placeholder can be moved to a different location. Also, if you are in the situation where you just need one more space to put the title in one line, then you can make the placeholder bigger. The placeholder is like a drawing object. Changing the size is the same as in a drawing object. When you make any changes to the placeholder in an individual slide, it affects only that particular slide.

Let's move the title box that has the text `Computer Hardware` in **Slide #1** somewhat higher.

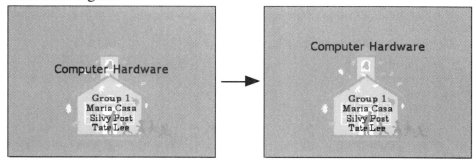

1. Click the title placeholder.
2. Drag it to the new location and drop it.

 ## Adding Graphics: Clip Arts and Pictures

Clip arts and pictures can be added at any location in the slide. Although you can choose the option to insert clip arts or pictures when you create a new slide, it is not required to insert them.

Insert a clip art or picture in Slide #2—Computer Hardware Components.
- Choose one that goes well with the background.
- Place it in the lower right corner. This will be linked to another slide in Activity 4.

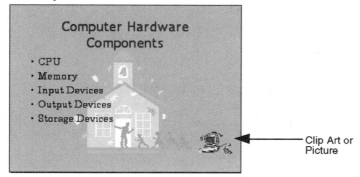

 ## Adding Movies

You can add movies in the PowerPoint™ presentation. The movies can be short digital movie clips or animated graphic files. Movies can be added from the **Insert** menu → **Movies and Sounds**.

NOTE On Macintosh, to access the full list of movies and sounds, the Value Pack should be installed on the hard drive from the MS Office program CD.

Let's add a movie to the first slide.

1. From the **Insert** menu → **Movies and Sounds** → **Movie from Gallery. . .** (Macintosh) / **Movie from Clip Organizer** (Windows).

2. Browse the movies.

3. To add a movie, click **Insert** (Macintosh) or click the movie icon (Windows).

4. Place the movie in the slide. For this activity, place the movie as in the following figure.

5. View the presentation to see the movie.

Adding Sounds

You can add sounds to the slide. The easiest way to add sounds is using the collection of sounds from MS Office. Also, you can use a music CD or record a sound. Sounds can be added from the **Insert** menu → **Movies and Sounds**.

Let's add a sound to the first slide.

1. From the **Insert** menu → **Movies and Sounds** → **Sound from Gallery. . .** (Macintosh) / **Sound from Clip Organizer** (Windows).

2. Browse the sounds.
   On Macintosh you can browse the sound first, on Windows you need to insert the sound first.

2-1. From the Gallery, click **Preview**.

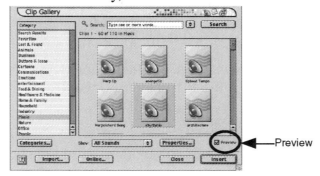

The Preview bar appears.

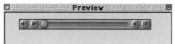

2-2. Click the sound that you want to listen to, once.
2-3. From the Preview bar play the sound.

The sounds with the music note icons have music, instead of short sound effects.

3. To add a sound, click **Insert** (Macintosh) or click the sound icon (Windows).

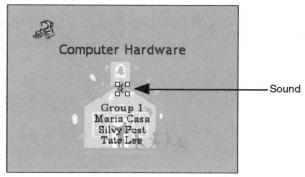

Click **NO** to the following message.

4. View the presentation to listen to the sound. Click the sound icon.

Adding Animation

Animation gives special effects to a slide element, such as how to appear or disappear.

Let's add animation to the two text placeholders in Slide #3 CPU.

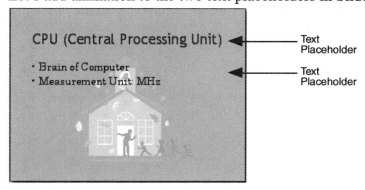

1. Let's add animation "Appear" to the Title CPU (Central Processiong Unit).

   1-1. Click the placeholder.
   1-2. Choose **Animations** from the **Slide Show** menu.
   1-3. Choose **Dissolve** as the animation effect.

   1-1. Click the placeholder.
   1-2. Choose **Custom Animations** from the **Slide Show** menu.
   1-3. From the **Add Effect** options, choose **Entrance → More Effects → Appear**.

   1-4. Click **OK**.

2. Add animation "Appear" to the second text placeholder.

3. Let's check the order of animation.
   There are two animations in this slide. To make sure which one comes first, use the custom animation.

   3-1. From the **Slide Show** menu, choose **Animations → Custom**.
   3-2. Choose the **Order and Timing** Tab. It should have the following order:

   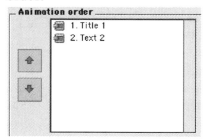

   If the order of the elements should be rearranged, select the element and click the arrow buttons in the left side of the dialog box to move up and down.

3-1. While you are in Custom Animation, check the order of animations, as in the following figure.

If the order of the elements should be rearranged, select the element and drag it up or down.

4. View the presentation.

Add the animation in Slide #4-8.

 Adding Custom Animation

As discussed in the previous section animation gives special effects to a slide element, such as how to appear or disappear. **Custom animation** is an advanced feature of animation that deals with all the elements of the slide.

Currently, in Slide #1 when you run the slide show, all the elements appear at the same time and disappear at the same time when you move to the next slide. The elements in the slide refer to the title text, text, clip art, movie, graphic object, or sound. For example, in Slide #1—Title Slide—there are four elements.

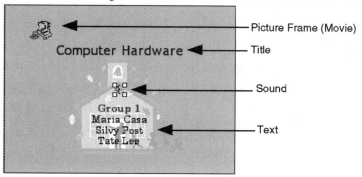

All these elements can be coordinated to give a dynamic presentation. Most custom animation options are the same between Windows and Macintosh. But there are some differences. For example, on Macintosh the effects can be added when the element enters the slide and exits the slide. On Windows it has to be when the element enters the slide or exits the slide, but not both.

Also, the Windows version has an option called "Motion Paths." Motion Paths is similar to effects but it creates a custom path of the element's moving path. The Motion Path is not available on Macintosh versions.

You don't have to use all the animation techniques that we will discuss here on one slide. However, adding some of these techniques can enhance the dynamics to your presentation.

You will add custom animation to Slide #1. When you finish the animation, the following effects will take place. Animations 1–5 are the same for Windows and Macintosh. Animation 6 is specific for each platform.

1. Slide #1 appears with the background and the sound icon.
2. Mouse click → Music plays.
3. Mouse click → Title `Computer Hardware` crawls in from the left.
4. Mouse click → Movie appears and plays.
5. Mouse click → Movie hides, and Text with names appears.

For Windows
6. Creating a Motion Path for the Movie

For Macintosh
6. The elements will fly out to right when exiting the slide.

Although you can achieve the same or similar animations between the Windows and the Macintosh versions, the steps are somewhat different. Therefore, two separate sets of instructions are provided. Follow the instructions for Macintosh or Windows.

> (CD) To browse the steps for this Adding Custom Animation section by viewing a movie, check out the file **CustAni-win** (Windows) or **CustAni-mac** (Macintosh) from the CD. (**Chapter 5** folder → **MoreInfo** folder → **CustAni-win** or **CustAni-mac**)

> (CD) To see the finished sample file for this Adding Custom Animation section, check out the file **PPT3 win** (Windows) or **PPT3 mac** (Macintosh) from the CD. (**Chapter 5** folder → **MoreInfo** folder)

Let's access the custom animation.

1. From the **Slide Show** menu, choose **Animation** → **Custom**. The Custom Animation dialog box appears.

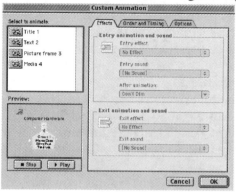

2. Let's identify the parts of the Custom Animation dialog box.
   - Do you see the elements of the slide? Title 1, Text 2, ... The number after each element indicates the order that was created.
   - The animation is controlled in the right side of the dialog box.
   - The Preview in the lower left allows you to see the animation that you apply without closing the dialog box.

Let's add Effects. The **effects** in custom animation control how each element enters the slide and exits the slide.

1. Choose the **Effects** tab.

2. Let's add Effects on the Title. The Title will crawl in from the left and fly out to the right.
   2-1. Select **Title 1**.
   2-2. Select the following effects:
      - Entry effect: **Crawl In From Left**
      - Exit effect: **Fly Out To Right**

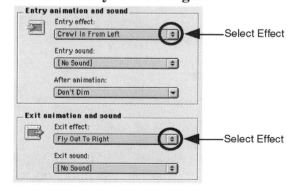

3. Let's add Effects on the Text—the group and names. The Text should appear and fly out to the right.
   3-1. Select **Text 2**.
   3-2. Select the following effects:
   - Entry effect: **Appear**
   - Exit effect: **Fly Out To Right**

4. Let's add Effects on the Movie. The movie will appear, hide when the next animation comes (when the Text with names appears), and fly out to the right.
   4-1. Select **Picture frame 3**.
   4-2. Select the following effects:
   - Entry effect: **Appear**
   - After animation: **Hide On Next Animation**
   - Exit effect: **Fly Out To Right**

5. Let's add Effects on the Sound. The Sound icon will be on the screen from the beginning and fly out to the right.
   5-1. Select **Media 4**.
   5-2. Select the following effects:
   - Entry effect: **No Effect** (No Effect means the element will be shown in the slide from the beginning.)
   - Exit effect: **Fly Out To Right**

Let's add Order and Timing. The **order and timing** in custom animation controls (a) the sequence of the elements' entrance to the slide and exit from the slide, and (b) the method of such events—by mouse clicking or automatic timing.

1. Choose the **Order and Timing** tab.

2. Let's organize the sequence.
   2-1. The following sequence in the Animation Order box is the correct sequence. To move the element, select the element and use the arrow buttons in the left side of the dialog box to move up and down.

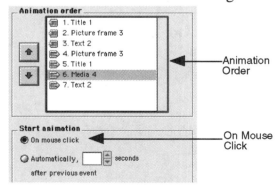

   2-2. Keep **On mouse click** for the Start Animation. That means the animation will be activated when the mouse is clicked.

Let's exit the custom animation and run the slide show.

1. Click **OK**.
2. Run the slide show.
   You will see the Sound icon in the slide. Don't forget to click it to play. Then, click the mouse to activate the next animation.

Let's access the custom animation.

1. From the **Slide Show** menu, choose **Custom Animation**.
   The Task Pane will show the Custom Animation options.

Let's add Effects. The **effects** in custom animation control how each element enters the slide and exits the slide.

1. Let's add Effects to the Title. The Title will crawl in from the left, very slowly.
   1-1. Select the title box of the title from the slide.
   1-2. From the **Add Effect** options, choose **Entrance → Crawl In**.

   1-3. From the **Direction** options, choose **From Left**.

   1-4. In the **Speed** Options, choose **Very Slow**.

   The animation will be entered in the Task Pane, and the animation number will be shown in the slide as a non-printing numbered list.

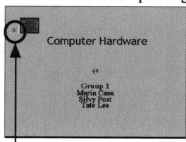

Non-printing numbered list

2. Add the following Effects to the Text—the group and names—to appear.
   - Entrance effect: **Appear**

3. Do not add any effect to the Sound. The Sound icon will be on the screen from the beginning.

4. Let's add Effects on the Movie. The movie should appear and hide when the next animation comes.
   - Entrance effect: **Appear**
   - After animation: **Hide on Next Mouse Click**

   To choose the **after animation** effect, use the following directions.

   4-1. Choose the Movie element and select **Effect Options. . . .**
        (The element number may be different from the following example, but you should see it in the list.)

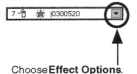

Choose **Effect Options**.

   4-2. From the Effect tab, choose **Hide on Next Mouse Click** for the **After animation** option.

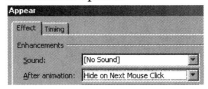

   4-3. Click **OK**.

5. View the presentation.

Let's add Order and Timing. The **order and timing** in custom animation controls (a) the sequence of the elements' entrance to the slide and exit from the slide, and (b) the method of such events—by mouse clicking or automatic timing.

In this activity, the "on click" (mouse click) was selected for timing, so keep it as it is.

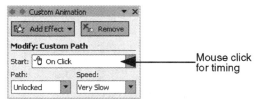

Mouse click for timing

The current order of animation is Sound (because it was not animated, it shows from the beginning) → Title → Text → Movie. Let's swap the sequence of the Text and the Movie, so the new sequence will be Sound → Title → Movie → Text. To change the sequence, move the Movie to a new location as in the following figure:

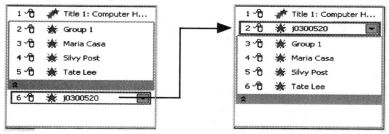

Let's try the Motion Paths.

1. Remove the current animation on the movie (because you need to add the Motion Paths).
   Click the Movie list from the Task Pane, and choose **Remove**.

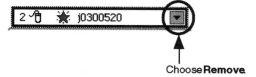

Choose **Remove**.

2. Click the Movie from the slide.

3. From the Task Pane, choose **Add Effect → Motion Paths → Draw Custom Path → Curve**.

   Of course, instead of the Curve, you can choose a different one. Also, you can use the predefined paths instead of drawing one yourself. For this activity, let's stay with the Curve.

4. To draw a path with the Curve tool:
   4-1. Click the movie.
   4-2. Draw a curved shape as you did with the drawing tool in Chapter 3.

4-3. To finish the curved shape, double-click where you want the last point to appear. In this example, put it somewhere at the end of the slide (see the following figure).

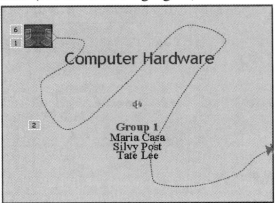

5. Change the Motion Paths speed to Very Slow:

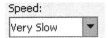

6. Place the Movie next to the Title.

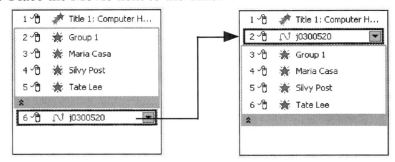

Adding Slide Transition

Slide transition is a visual and/or sound effect added when advancing from one slide to another.

Let's add slide transition to the presentation.
(If you don't like it, you can delete the transition later.)

1. Choose **Slide Transition. . .** from the **Slide Show** menu.
   The dialog box appears on Macintosh; on Windows, the Task Pane changes.

2. Choose an Effect and Speed.

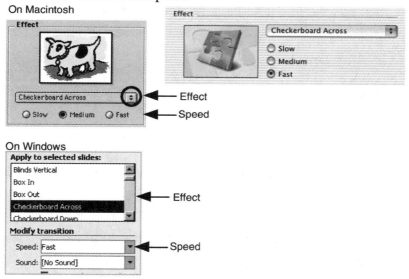

3. Choose whether to apply the transition to the current slide only or to all the slides.

   Click **Apply** or **Apply to all**.

   Apply will apply the transition effect only to the selected slide. **Apply to all** will apply to all the slides.

   To apply to the current slide only, don't do anything. Just choose the transition. To apply to all the slides, click **Apply to All Slides**.

4. Keep **On mouse click** for Advance.

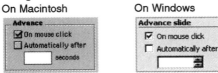

5. You can choose Sound effect only very sparingly. (Imagine how distracting it would be, if every slide had a clapping sound.)

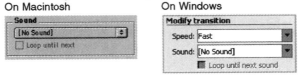

6. View the presentation to see the transition effect.

Finishing Touches

Save the file.

Project 3

This project is to format the presentation developed in Project 2.

1. Open the file **PR2**.
2. Save the file as **PR3**.
3. Add new slides—about 3 or 4 slides—to finish the contents for the Food Guide Pyramid.
4. Format the presentation:
   • Add indentation, when needed. (Demote the text.)
   • Adjust paragraph spacing, when needed.
   • Add a clip art or a picture.
   • Add a movie or an animated graphic.
   • Add sound.
   • Apply animation to text.
   • Apply custom animation on at least one slide.
   • Add slide transitions.
5. Save the file.

Activity 4: Formatting Presentation II

In this activity the PowerPoint™ presentation formatted in Activity 3 will be enhanced by adding an organization chart and creating non-linear navigations. Also, the presentation will be saved as web page and QuickTime™ movie.

File needed for this activity: PRESENTATION3

This activity will guide you through the following tasks:

- Working with an organization chart
- Non-linear navigation: Understanding non-linear navigation
- Non-linear navigation: Creating links with slide objects
- Non-linear navigation: Creating links with buttons
- Adding notes
- Printing a PowerPoint™ document
- Saving as Web page
- Saving as QuickTime™ movie

Before You Begin

1. Open PRESENTATION3.

2. Save the file as PRESENTATION4.
   Save the file often during the activity.

Working with an Organization Chart

An organization chart can be added by choosing the Organization Chart slide.

Let's add a slide with an organization chart describing the computer hardware components. When finished, the slide will be similar to the following figure. On both

Windows and Macintosh you can make the same chart, but the steps are somewhat different. Therefore, separate instructions are provided.

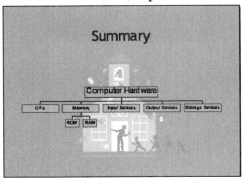

1. Insert a new slide with Organization Chart layout. The new slide will be the second-last slide.

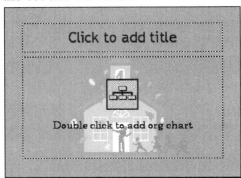

2. Double-click to add an organization chart.
   The organization chart screen appears:

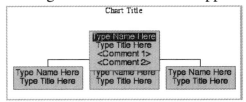

3. The finished chart should be as follows:

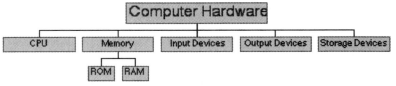

To enter text, type where it says **Type Name Here**.
Ignore the brackets <Comment 1> or <Comment 2>.

4. To add a box use the following tools.
   Subordinate creates a box in a lower hierarchy, **Co-worker** in an equal level, and **Manager** in a higher hierarchy.

5. When the organization chart is complete, choose **Quit and Return to Presentation 4 (or Update and Return to Presentation 4)** from the **File** menu.
   The organization chart will be placed in the slide.

1. Insert a new slide with Organization Chart layout. The new slide will be the second-last slide.

2. Choose Organization Chart from the dialog box.

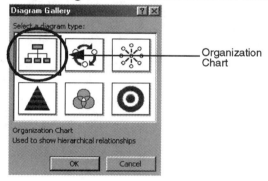

Organization Chart

3. Click **OK**.
   The diagram layout appears.

4. The finished chart should be as follows:

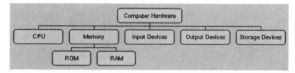

- To enter text, click inside the box and type.
- To add a box, use the **Insert Shape** tab. **Subordinate** creates a box in a lower hierarchy and **Co-worker** in an equal level.

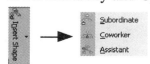

Non-Linear Navigation: Understanding Non-Linear Navigation

So far the presentation is going from one slide to the next or to the previous one. That is **linear navigation**. Linear presentation navigates the slides to immediately adjacent slides. On the other hand, **non-linear navigation** is designed to go to any slide regardless of the physical sequence.

For example, from Slide #2—Computer Hardware Components—you can launch different parts of the presentation as in the following figure.

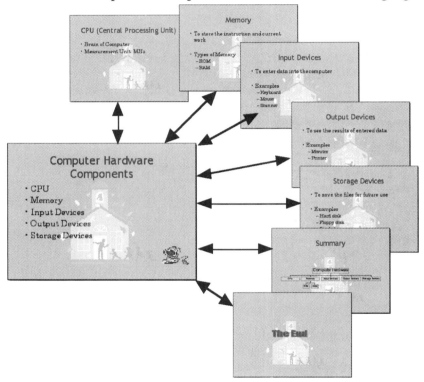

Even after adding the non-linear navigation, you can still use the presentation as the linear presentation. Creating a non-linear navigation takes time but it can give more dynamics to the presentation. When you use one location to show all the topics to be covered, as you come back to the screen the audience has a better understanding about what was covered and what needs to be covered. Also, after the presentation, when you answer questions, you can refer to the section quickly without going through all the slides.

> **CD** Non-linear Navigation will be discussed in the next two sections. To see the finished sample file for these sections, check out the file **PPT4** from the CD. (**Chapter 5** folder → **MoreInfo** folder)

Non-Linear Navigation: Creating Links with Slide Objects

Linking (or **Hyperlinking**) a slide element means to activate the element to go to a particular slide. The common slide objects for linking are text, clip art, picture, and drawing object.

You will link the slide objects in Slide #2 for non-linear presentation. Here is the plan:
- Text **CPU** → Slide #3
- Text **Memory** → Slide #4 (Memory)
- Text **Input Devices** → Slide #6 (Input Devices)
- Text **Output Devices** → Slide #7 (Output Devices)
- Text **Storage Devices** → Slide #8 (Storage Devices)
- Clip art → Slide #9 (Summary)

Let's link text **CPU** in Slide #2 to go to Slide #3.

1. Select the text **CPU**.

2. Choose **Action Settings. . .** from the **Slide Show** menu.
   Action Settings dialog box appears.

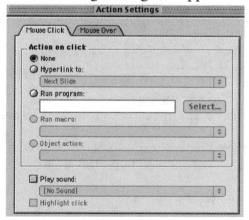

3. Select **Mouse Click** Tab as in the preceding figure.
   Mouse Click means the action will take place when the mouse is clicked.

4. Click **Hyperlink to:** from the **Action on click**.
   "Hyperlink to:" means that the selected object will be linked.

5. Select **Slide. . .** from the **Hyperlink to:** options.

6. Click on the slide to be linked. In this case, it is Slide #3 `CPU (Central Processing Unit)`.

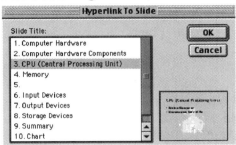

7. Click **OK**. Click **OK** again.

The text is hyperlinked. When text is hyperlinked, its color changes and its style becomes underlined.

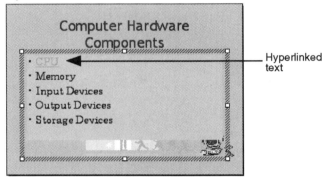

8. View the presentation to test the link.

Once the hyperlink is visited, it becomes **followed hyperlink**.

Sometimes the followed hyperlink color does not go well with the background. It can be changed. Let's change the followed hyperlink color.

1. Let's access the color scheme.

    1-1. Choose **Slide Color Scheme. . .** from the **Format** menu.
    1-2. Choose the **Custom** Tab.

    1-1. From the Formatting Toolbar, choose **Design**.

    1-2. From the Task Pane, choose **Color Schemes**.

    🔲 Color Schemes

1-3. Choose **Edit Color Schemes** at the end of the Task Pane.

Edit Color Schemes...

1-4. Choose the **Custom** Tab.

2. Click **Accent and followed hyperlink**.

Click here.

3. Click **Change Color** button.

4. Choose color. And then, click **OK**.

5. Click **Apply**.

Complete the following links in Slide #2:
- Text **Memory** → Slide #4 (Memory)
- Text **Input Devices** → Slide #6 (Input Devices)
- Text **Output Devices** → Slide #7 (Output Devices)
- Text **Storage Devices** → Slide #8 (Storage Devices)
- Clip art → Slide #9 (Summary)

When finished, Slide #2 will be similar to the following figure:

Non-Linear Navigation: Creating Links with Buttons

By the end of the previous section, the links from Slide #2 are finished to launch to other slides (topics). In order to complete the non-linear navigation, there should be a way to come back to Slide #2. For example, from `Output Devices` slide, it should be possible to come back to Slide #2.

There is no slide object to add such a navigation. So, you will add an object—a button.

Let's add a button in Slide #3—`CPU`—to come back to Slide #2.

1. In Slide #3, add a button from the AutoShapes (from the Drawing Toolbar).
   If you happened to choose a shape from the Action Buttons, the hyperlink dialog box comes up automatically. Cancel to close the hyperlink for now.

Action Button

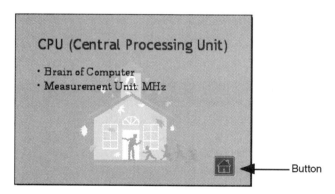

Button

2. Change the color of the button to match with the background.

3. Hyperlink the button to go to Slide #2.
   (Use Slide Show menu → Action Settings. . . .)

4. View the presentation to test the link.

There are several places that you need a button to go back to Slide #2. You have just created one in Slide #3. Since the function is the same—to go to Slide #2—it is possible to copy the button and use it again.

Copy the newly created button and paste it in the following slides:

Slide #5

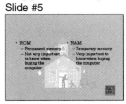

Slide #6

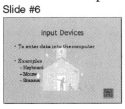

Slide #7

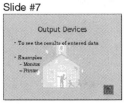

Slide #8

Slide #9

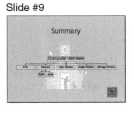

Slide #11

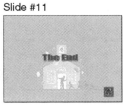

While you paste the button, if the following message appears, check "Don't tell me about masters again." Then, click **OK**.

Put an object on all slides

You can put an object on every slide in your presentation by putting it on the slide master.

- Put this object on the slide master
- Take me to the slide master
- Tell me about the slide master

☑ Don't tell me about masters again

OK

It is good to use the Slide Master if the button should be placed in every slide. It is your decision whether to place the button to go back to the starting point on every slide or not. Sometimes it is effective to put the button on every slide. But in this example, we placed the button at the end of each topic. Most topics have only one slide in this activity, however, the topics can consist of more than one slide.

Adding Notes

Notes in PowerPoint™ presentation is for the presenter's information, which can include more information, how to explain the ideas, or a simple reminder. It can be printed along with the slides so that the presenter can use this information when preparing the presentation. Also, if you use the same presentation at a later time, the notes will remind you of the presentation plan.

Let's add a note in Slide #1 as a reminder to click the sound icon first.

1. Be in Slide #1.

2. Type your note in the box, `Click the sound icon first!`

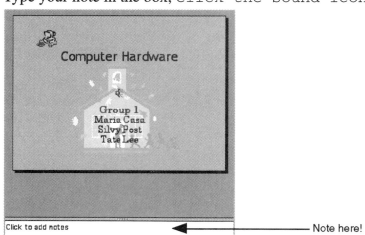

3. To see the notes, you can also choose **Notes Page** from the **View** menu.

4. Choose **Normal** from the **View** menu to come back to the slide.

Let's add a note on Slide #3 for detailed information about CPU. You can copy the text from WORD4 and paste it in the note box.

 Printing a PowerPoint™ Document

You can print a PowerPoint™ document with different styles—one slide per page, two, three, or six slides per page, or with notes. When you distribute a handout, three slides per page would be good. If you want to reduce the number of the printed pages, six slides would be the choice. For your own copy of the presentation, print it with notes.

Printing a PowerPoint™ document is accessible from **Print. . .** from the **File** menu.

Let's print the presentation—6 slides per page. See the separate instructions for Windows and Macintosh.

1. Choose **Print. . .** from the **File** menu.

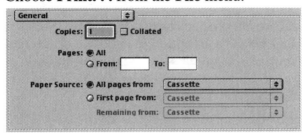

This is a typical printing dialog box. If you print from this dialog box, one slide will be printed per page. This is not the usual way to print a presentation file.

2. Choose **Microsoft PowerPoint** from the options.

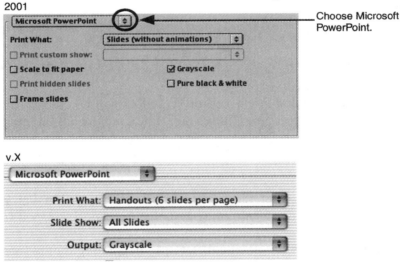

3. Choose **Handouts (6 slides per page)**.

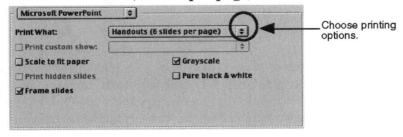

4. Click **Print**.

1. Choose **Print...** from the **File** menu.

2. Choose **Handouts** for **Print What**, and **6** for **Slides per page**.

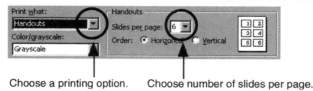

Choose a printing option.   Choose number of slides per page.

Print What is to choose the format of printing. Slides will print the slide per page. Handouts has an option to choose a different number of slides per page. Notes will print the slide with your notes.

3. Click **OK**.

 Saving as a Web Page

Before working on this section, save the current file.

You can save the PowerPoint™ presentation as web page. Let's save the file as web page:

1. Choose **Save As Web Page...** from the **File** menu.

2. Give the file name as **PresentationWeb.htm** and choose the file format as **Web Page**.
   The file titled **PresentationWeb.htm** will be created, along with the folder **PresentationWeb_files**. The folder contains all the necessary files.

PresentationWeb.htm   PresentationWeb_files

3. To view the web page, open the file **PresentationWeb.htm** from an Internet browser program. Usually, by choosing Open from the File menu.

The web page may be viewed differently depending on the Internet browser. Also, the web page can be viewed by choosing Web Page Preview from the File menu. This will prompt the default Internet browser.

 Saving as a QuickTime™ Movie

Saving the PowerPoint™ presentation as a QuickTime™ movie is a new feature in MS Office, and it is available only on Macintosh. It translates the presentation file into a QuickTime™ movie that can be opened with QuickTime™ Player on both Windows and Macintosh computers. (To get the most current version of Quick-Time™ Player, visit http://www.apple.com/quicktime.)

A QuickTime™ movie is a linear presentation, not for clicking the non-linear links. Therefore, you cannot use the links or listen to the sound that you added. But the quality of the graphic and text in the movie is good. If you are on Macintosh, try it. If you are on Windows, open the converted movie file, **PresentationQT**.

 To see a translated QuickTime™ movie, check out the file **PresentationQT** from the CD. (**Chapter 5** folder → **MoreInfo** folder → **PresentationQT**)

To save the presentation as a QuickTime™ movie (only on Macintosh):

MAC

1. Choose **Make Movie. . .** from the **File** menu.

2. Name the file **PresentationQT**, and check **Append file extension**.

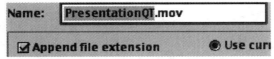

   File extension for QuickTime™ movie is .mov. The extension is not necessary on Macintosh, but it is essential on Windows. In order to run the movie on both platforms, add the extension.

3. Click **Save**.

4. If you come up with a dialog box, click **OK**. Otherwise, the file has been converted into a movie.

5. Open the file **PresentationQT** to watch the QuickTime™ movie.

Project 4

This project is to format the presentation developed in Project 3.

1. Open the file **PR3**.
2. Save the file as **PR4**.
3. Add an organization chart to organize food group information.
4. Create a non-linear navigation.
   It should have a starting point and the navigation should be completed to come back to this starting point from different slides.
   • Link at least one text.
   • Link at least one clip art or picture.
   • Create and link at least one button.
5. Save the file.
6. Save the file as web page. The file name is **PR4Web.htm**.
7. (Macintosh only) Save the file as a QuickTime™ movie. The file name is **PR4QT.mov**.

Integration with Other Programs

Integration of a presentation program with other application programs is somewhat similar to word processing. Word processing is for printed materials, while a presentation program is for computer-based presentation.

Inserting a graphic into a presentation document is the most common integration with other programs. The graphic can be drawing, painting, clip arts, images developed with other graphic programs, scanned pictures, and digital photos from a digital camera. Another kind of graphic is the chart created in a spreadsheet program.

In addition to graphic, animations and movie clips can be added in the presentation. Developing an animation or a movie clip is not part of the presentation program; therefore, it should be developed with other programs and integrated into the presentation.

Also, spreadsheet data—those in columns and rows—can be copied and pasted into a presentation. In this case, the data will be converted into a graphic. Therefore, it is only for viewing, not for editing the data.

Text from a word processing file can be integrated into a presentation. However, it is not recommended that the presenter have a long text to read in the presentation, unless there is a particular purpose for doing it. But it is useful to keep detailed notes (by adding notes to the presentation) for the presenter's information.

Applications

In this chapter, the hands-on skills for creating presentations and the ideas for using presentation tools in the classroom were discussed. Examine the possibilities of applying presentation tools in education.

1. Collect ideas on how to use presentation programs with the students. You can refer to the *Getting Started* section to create your own ideas.

2. Collect ideas on how to use presentation programs as a teacher for classroom management and teaching. You can refer to the *Getting Started* section to create your own ideas. Consider the following example to get started:

Example

Activity Purpose: To develop presentation for teaching.
Activity Description: Teachers can develop presentations for teaching. See the following examples from the CD.

- **Internet**
- **The Shurley™ English Sentence Jingle** [file name: Sentence]

 (**Chapter 5** folder → **Applications** folder)

---

3. Create a lesson plan in which you can integrate presentation programs by expanding the ideas in the section *Getting Started* or by developing your own ideas. Include the following components:
   - Subject matter
   - Grade level
   - Purpose of the activity (lesson objective)
   - Target audience
     - Prior knowledge on the lesson objective (any related content covered?)
     - Computer skill
     - Any other information that you want to include
   - Environment
     - Location: In the classroom or in the lab?
     - Number of computers needed
   - Description of instructional activity
     - Description on how the lesson will proceed and how a presentation program will be used

4. Collect ideas on how to integrate presentation programs with other programs. You can refer to the section *Integration with Other Programs* to create your own ideas.

Summary

1. PowerPoint™ is a popular presentation program.

2. There are various applications of the presentation tools in education for students and teachers.

3. From the hands-on activities for creating presentation, the following tasks were covered:
   - Creating a presentation
     - Using templates
     - Designing the Slide Master and the background
     - Working with text
     - Adding and deleting slides
     - Browsing the slides
     - Viewing the presentation
     - Rearranging the slides
     - Formatting text: Paragraph spacing, Indentation
     - Formatting Text Placeholders
     - Working with an organization chart
   - Making the presentation more dynamic
     - Adding graphics, movies, sounds, animation, custom animation, slide transitions
     - Creating non-linear navigation
   - Notes and printing
     - Adding notes
     - Printing a PowerPoint™ document
   - Transforming the PowerPoint™ presentation
     - Saving as web page
     - Saving as QuickTime™ movie

Chapter 6

Database Techniques Using Excel

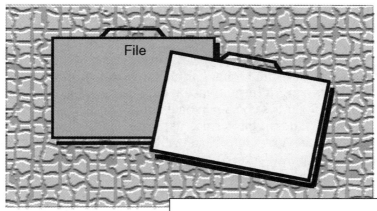

File

Getting Started
Activity 1: Using Spreadsheet as a
     Database
  Project 1
Activity 2: Data Merge
  Project 2
Integration with Other Programs
Applications
Summary

Getting Started

 ## Features of a Database

Database is a computer program for organizing information. It resembles a folder in a file cabinet or a rolodex with addresses. Database is a computerized filing system or record-keeping system.

There are many examples of databases around us. When you go to a library the collection—books, magazines, journals, videotapes, audiotapes, DVDs, and so on—is classified in the computer catalog system, and you can search the items. This computer catalog system is a database. Let's think about another example. Your school record is stored in the computer. The record may contain your name, address, date of birth, courses that you have taken, and grades. Think about the number of students enrolled each year, and that the school needs to keep all the information for years to come. The database could contain extensive information.

The database that we will use in the classroom may not be as big as the library computer catalog system or the school's student information system. However, it is very useful for organizing information for the students and the teachers. This scaled-down version of database on a personal computer level is often called a "filing system." In reality, though, the terms "database" and "filing system" in the personal computer level are used interchangeably. Therefore, some programs are named *database* (e.g., AppleWorks™) and some are named *file* (e.g., File Maker Pro™). In this book we will stay with the term "database."

The features of database can be summarized as follows:

- **Fields**. The first thing to do when creating a database is to define fields. A field is the place to hold specific information in database such as last name, first name, and so on. The decision on what information should be collected is made in this process.

- **Records**. A **record** is one set of information collected in the fields. For example, one student's information such as last name, first name, address, parents' name(s), telephone number, and date of birth is one record.

- **Sorting records**. The records can be sorted in descending or ascending order by any field.

- **Finding records**. The information can be searched.

- **Matching records**. The records that match the selection criteria can be found. For example, find all the records that have a score higher than 90 points.

- **Hiding and showing records**. It is possible to build up a large database and use only a few data (records) at a given time by hiding the rest. Also, the hidden data (records) can be shown again.

- **Appearance**. It is possible to change the appearance of the database, for example, by adding a background color or moving the location of fields.

- **Layout**. There are several options for the layouts. It is possible to keep more than one layout for one database.

A database program is available as a stand-alone program (e.g., Claris File Maker Pro™, Microsoft Access™) or as part of integrated software, such as Apple-Works™ or MicrosoftWorks™. Once you have learned how to use a database with any of these programs, you should be able to apply your knowledge to other database programs.

Databases, Spreadsheets, and Microsoft Office™

In this chapter, the spreadsheet program Excel™ will be used as a database. As we discussed earlier, the primary applications of spreadsheet are to deal with numerical data. The secondary function of spreadsheet is its use as a simple database. The real database in MS Office™ is Access™.

There are two reasons why Access™ was not adopted for this book. One is the availability of the program. Access™ is available only for Windows computers—not for Macintosh computers. Even for the Windows versions, it does not come with the Standard version of MS Office™. It is available only in the Professional version and the Developer version. Considering that the Standard version of MS Office™ is available for teachers and students at an education price, the availability of Access™ is somewhat limited, not to mention the Macintosh users. The other reason is that Excel™ can provide adequate coverage for simple database tasks.

It is possible to conduct most database tasks with Excel™—creating a database, sorting data, and creating data merge (mail merge or creating personalized letters). Storing simple data is ideal when you use Excel™ as a database such as names, phone numbers, e-mail addresses, and so on. A limitation of using Excel™ as a database is that the formatting of a database is limited to the appearance of the spreadsheet. Therefore, it is impossible to have a field to type long text or to keep graphics. The following examples compare the databases on student projects developed with a spreadsheet and with a database program.

Database with a spreadsheet program

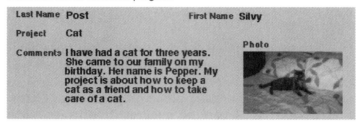

Database with a database program

Databases in Teaching and Learning

The primary applications of database are to organize the data. A few examples of how students can use database are as follows:

- Data classification
  - Students can classify information on the solar system by the planets, sources of information (book, Web sites, reference materials, magazines), content of information, and photos.
  - Students can classify food items according to the food groups, nutrition factor, serving sizes, and photos of the food items.
  - Students can classify animals by categories (mammals, birds, insects, and reptiles), favorite food, hibernation, and other information.
  - Students can classify information on the United States by the individual states, their capitals, state flowers, population, and other comments. This geography database can be extended to the international level by country, the country's capital, and so forth.

- Group data collection
  - Students can organize their class yearbook data.
  - Students can organize their art collections—student names, titles, and artifacts (computer graphics, digitized photographs).
  - Students can create book reports individually and combine all the reports as a class project.

- Journal
  - Students can keep information on their field trip—what they learned from the field trip and the related subject area.

Teachers can use database for instructional activities with the students' participation as indicated in the preceding examples. Also, teachers can use database for instructional material development and for classroom management as follows:

- Instructional resource
  - Teachers can teach organization skills to classify the information. For example, teachers can create a database, discuss how to classify the information, and ask the students to fill in the rest of the database based on their findings. The topic could be the solar system, animals, or rocks, to list a few.
  - Teachers can use a database as a problem-solving tool. For example, a database can be used to list hypotheses (or questions), possible resources to find the answers, and the answers found.
  - Teachers can have the recommended reading list cataloged and note the books that are available in the classroom.
  - Teachers can keep a database on educational resources from the World Wide Web. The information can be classified as the titles of the sites, URLs, related subject matter, target audience, contents of the sites, and the teacher's evaluation for future use in class.
  - Teachers can create a test bank.

- Administrative use
  - Teachers can keep students' records such as parents' names, contact information, addresses, and other important information.
  - Teachers can keep track of students' portfolios.
  - Teachers can organize the information necessary for field trips.

Overview of This Chapter

Activities and Projects

There are two activities for creating a database with Excel™ and using it for data merge. After each activity a project is provided to apply what was covered in the activity.

Applications, Integration with Other Programs, and Summary

At the end of the chapter, the Applications section can be used for brainstorming and developing ideas to use database techniques in teaching and learning. Integration with Other Programs and Summary sections follow.

Icons to Watch

WIN **MAC** There are a few differences between the Windows and Macintosh versions. When a different instruction is required, it is indicated by the corresponding icons.

CD When there is a file on the CD that you can check, it is indicated with the icon.

More Information

It is recommended to complete Chapter 4 "Microsoft Excel: The Spreadsheet Tool" before this chapter.

Activity 1: Using Spreadsheet as a Database

In this activity a database will be created with Excel™ to enter students' project data and parents' information.

This activity will guide you through the following tasks:

- Setting up a database
- Understanding database structure
- Filling in the form
- Sorting data
- Filtering data with AutoFilter
- Filtering data with Custom Filter
- Showing All Records

Before You Begin

Create a new Excel™ document.

 ### Setting Up a Database

Setting up a database in Excel™ is the same as using it as a spreadsheet. Enter the data as follows:

	A	B	C	D	E	F	G
1	Last Name	First Name	Group	Project Title	Score	Parent's Name	Salute
2	Casa	Maria	Group 1	Computer Use in English	90	Casa	Mr.
3	Post	Silvy	Group 1	Computer Use in history	95	Post	Ms.
4	Lee	Tate	Group 1	Computer Use in science	93	Lee	Mr. & Mrs.

➲ Understanding Database Structure

Currently, your database has three records. Let's take a look at the structure of your database as described in the following diagram:

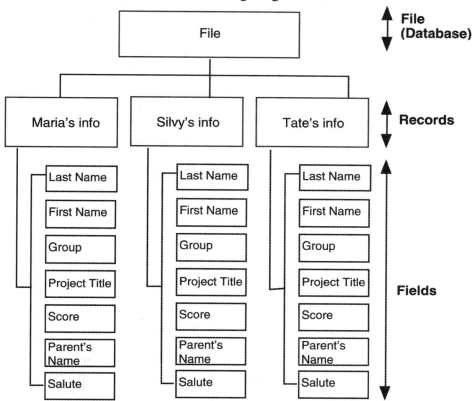

A **field** in a database contains specific information, such as a last name or a first name. A field contains `Casa`, `Maria`, `Group 1`, `Computer Use in English`, `90`, `Casa`, or `Mr`. It is the same as what each cell contains in this Excel™-based database. A collection of fields makes a **record**. A record is the same as one row. In this example, all the fields for Maria's information make one record. A collection of records makes a **file**. In the personal computer level, a file is considered a database.

➲ Filling in the Form

The data in spreadsheet format can be translated into a **form**, which looks similar to a typical database. Let's change the format of the data into the form:

1. Select the cells that have data—from Cell A1 to G4.

2. Choose **Form. . .** from the **Data** menu.
   The form will be created.

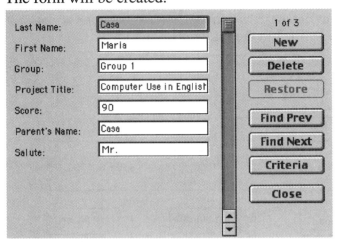

3. Browse the data by using the scroll bar or the buttons **Find Prev** and **Find Next**.

4. The data can also be entered in the form. Let's add a new set of data.
   4-1. Click **New**.
   4-2. Enter data as follows:

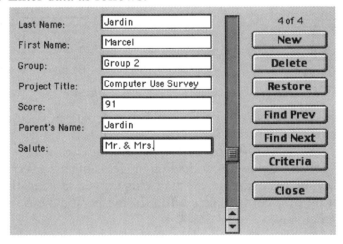

5. Let's go back to the spreadsheet format. Click **Close**.
   The new data are shown in the spreadsheet.

	A	B	C	D	E	F	G
1	**Last Name**	**First Name**	**Group**	**Project Title**	**Score**	**Parent's Name**	**Salute**
2	Casa	Maria	Group 1	Computer Use in English	90	Casa	Mr.
3	Post	Silvy	Group 1	Computer Use in history	95	Post	Ms.
4	Lee	Tate	Group 1	Computer Use in science	93	Lee	Mr. & Mrs.
5	Jardin	Marcel	Group 2	Computer Use Survey	91	Jardin	Mr. & Mrs.

Sorting Data

The data can be sorted as usual. Sort the data according to the **descending order of Score** as follows:

	A	B	C	D	E	F	G
1	**Last Name**	**First Name**	**Group**	**Project Title**	**Score**	**Parent's Name**	**Salute**
2	Post	Silvy	Group 1	Computer Use in history	95	Post	Ms.
3	Lee	Tate	Group 1	Computer Use in science	93	Lee	Mr. & Mrs.
4	Jardin	Marcel	Group 2	Computer Use Survey	91	Jardin	Mr. & Mrs.
5	Casa	Maria	Group 1	Computer Use in English	90	Casa	Mr.

 ## Filtering Data with AutoFilter

Filtering data is selecting records by criteria and hiding the records that do not meet the criteria. **AutoFilter** sets up the criteria within each field, and the records that meet the criteria will remain while the rest will be hidden.

Let's select the records by group—show only Group 1 and hide the others.

1. Select the cells that have data—from Cell A1 to G5.

2. From the **Data** menu, choose **Filter → AutoFilter**.
   The **Sorter and Filter** icon will be added to the field name in the database:

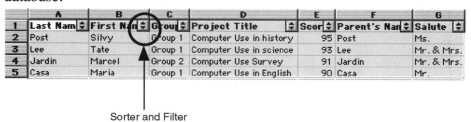

Sorter and Filter

3. To show only Group 1, click the **Sorter and Filter** icon from **Group**, and choose **Group 1**.

On Macintosh

On Windows

4. Examine the records.
Some records are hidden, and the Sorter and Filter icon of the Group has changed the color.

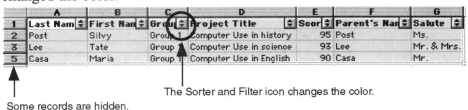

	A	B	C	D	E	F	G
1	Last Nam ⬍	First Nam ⬍	Grou ⬍	Project Title ⬍	Scor ⬍	Parent's Nam ⬍	Salute ⬍
2	Post	Silvy	Group 1	Computer Use in history	95	Post	Ms.
3	Lee	Tate	Group 1	Computer Use in science	93	Lee	Mr. & Mrs.
5	Casa	Maria	Group 1	Computer Use in English	90	Casa	Mr.

The Sorter and Filter icon changes the color.

Some records are hidden.

Filtering Data with Custom Filter

Custom Filter is the mechanism to filter the records within the AutoFilter with the user-defined criteria. Before filtering with Custom Filter, you have to be in Auto-Filter.

Currently, only Group 1 records are shown. Let's filter the records that have a score higher than 92 within Group 1.

1. From the **Sorter and Filter** icon from the **Score**, choose **Custom Filter** or **Custom. . .**, as in the following figure.

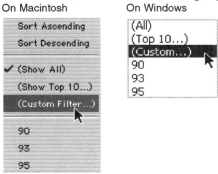

On Macintosh   On Windows

2. From the Custom AutoFilter dialog box, fill in the criteria as follows—remember that you are filtering the records that have a score higher than **92**.

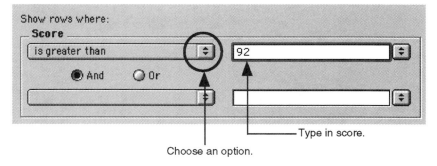

Choose an option.   Type in score.

3. Click **OK**.
   The newly filtered database will be shown.

	A	B	C	D	E	F	G
1	Last Nam	First Nam	Grou	Project Title	Scor	Parent's Nar	Salute
2	Post	Silvy	Group 1	Computer Use in history	95	Post	Ms.
3	Lee	Tate	Group 1	Computer Use in science	93	Lee	Mr. & Mrs.
6							
7							

 ## Showing All Records

Showing All Records shows all the records in the database. In order to do so, the records should be shown from one Sorter and Filter icon at a time. In this activity, there are two Sorter and Filter icons that have filtered the records—Group and Score.

Let's show all records.

1. Let's show all records from Group.
   1-1. Choose the Sorter and Filter icon of **Group**.
   1-2. Choose **Show All** or **All**.

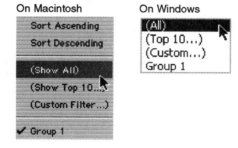

2. Show all records from Score.

   All records will be shown.

Finishing Touches

Save the file as DATABASE1.

Project 1

In this project you will create a database of the food groups.

1. Create a database document.

2. Enter eight records that are listed below.

Food Item	Food Group
White bread	Bread
Apple	Fruit
Cherry	Fruit
Tomato	Vegetable
Cheddar cheese	Milk
Salmon	Meat
Chicken	Meat
Salad dressing	Fats

3. Filter the records to show the Fruit group only.

4. Save the document as **DB1**.

> **CD** To see a finished sample project, check out the file **DB-Proj1** from the CD. (**Chapter 5** folder → **Projects** folder → **DB-Proj1**)

Activity 2: Data Merge

This activity is based on the following scenario:

"From Activity 1, a database was created to collect students' project information and parents' contact information. The teacher wants to notify the parents regarding the exhibition of the students' work. The teacher wants to send out the note with personalized information such as the student's name, the title of the project, and the parents' names."

This is when to use data merge to generate the same note with the personalized information inserted. In this activity, the custom letters—form letters—will be created. In Project 2, following Activity 2, the labels will be generated with data merge.

This activity will guide you through the following tasks:

- Understanding data merge
- Preparing a word processing document
- Preparing a database file
- Merging data: Creating form letters

 ## Understanding Data Merge

Data merge is creating customized letters, labels, or envelopes in a word processing file by inserting information from a database file. Creating customized letters—form letters—is also referred to as **mail merge**. For example, when a teacher is preparing a letter to the parents, the content of the letter is the same for all the parents. However, the students' names and the parents' names will be different. This unique information will be saved in a database and inserted into the letter. It is not necessary to type a letter for individual parents. The computer will combine the contents of the letter and the unique information and then print the customized letters.

To create data merge, a word processing file and a database file are needed. It is also possible to create the data source within Word™ only for the data merge. However, that data source cannot be used for a general purpose of database. In this activity, a new letter will be generated with Word™ and the file DATABASE 1 will be used.

 ## Preparing a Word Processing File

1. Create a new Word™ document, and prepare a letter as follows.

Do NOT type the double brackets (« ») and the information inside the double brackets! These are the field names that will be merged from the database file.

Today's Date

```
Dear «Salute» «Parent's Name»,

I am glad to inform you that «First Name»'s project
will be displayed in the Student Project Fair of the
year. The title of the project is «Title». The
exhibition schedule will be announced later. If you
have any questions or if you can volunteer, please
contact me. Your support is very important to us.

Sincerely,
```

Your name, Chair
Student Project Fair

2. Save the document as LETTER.

Preparing a Database File

In this activity, the database file DATABASE1 that was created with Excel™ will be used. When the database file is merged into Word™ document, the filtering and sorting result will not be carried over. Therefore, if the records should be filtered or sorted, it should be done after the data source is imported. In this activity, the letters will be sent out only to the parents of Group 1.

Merging Data: Creating Form Letters

Merging data is to combine the word processing text and the information from the data source. In this section a set of form letters will be created. On both Windows and Macintosh you can achieve the same results. The commands to be used are about the same. However, there are slight differences between the two platforms. Therefore, two separate instructions are provided.

1. Let's have the right tools available.
   From the **Tools** menu, choose **Data Merge Manager**.

2. While you are in the file LETTER, choose **Data Merge Manager** dialog box → **Main Document** → **Create** → **Form Letters**.

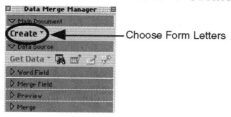

—Choose Form Letters

3. Let's get the data source—DATABASE1.
   3-1. From the **Data Merge Manager**, click **Get Data**.

   3-2. Choose **Open Data Source**.
   3-3. Find DATABASE1.
   3-4. In the Open Worksheet dialog box, keep the information as follows:

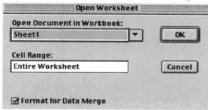

   3-5. Click **OK**.
      The fields will be imported in the **Data Merge Manager** → **Merge Field**.

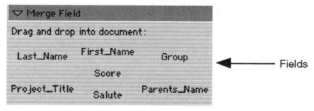

— Fields

4. Let's merge the fields in the letter.
   4-1. Drag the Salute field to the place of **«Salute»** and drop it.

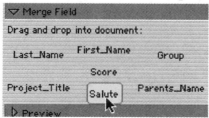

      The field will be inserted in the letter.

```
Dear «Salute»
```

      Be careful with spacing. There should a space between **Dear** and **«Salute»**.

4-2. Merge the **Parent Name** field in the appropriate place of the letter. Don't forget the correct spacing!

4-3. Merge the **First Name** field in the appropriate place of the letter.

4-4. Merge the **Project Title** field in the appropriate place of the letter.

5. Let's filter the records and select only Group 1.

5-1. In the Data Merge Manager, choose **Merge →Query Options. . . .**

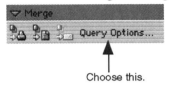

Choose this.

5-2. Choose **Filter Records** tab.

5-3. Choose the options as in the following figure.

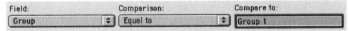

5-4. Click **OK**.

6. Save the file LETTER.

7. Let's generate a new document and save the merged letters. You filtered the records to select Group 1 only. There were three records for Group 1. Therefore, three letters will be generated within one file.

7-1. In the Data Merge Manager, choose **Merge to New Document** under **Merge**.

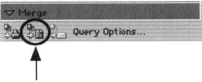

Merge to New Document

7-2. Browse the letters.

7-3. Save the letters as MERGEDLETTER.

 WIN

1. (While you are in the file LETTER) Let's have the right tools available. From the **Tools** menu, choose **Letters and Mailings → Show Mail Merge Toolbar**.

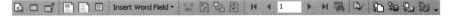

2. Let's set up the main document.

2-1. From the **Mail Merge Toolbar**, choose **Main Document Set Up**.

2-2. Choose **Letter** as the Main Document Type.

2-3. Click **OK**.

3. Let's get the data source—DATABASE1.

    3-1. From the **Mail Merge Toolbar** choose **Open Data Source**.

    3-2. Find DATABASE1.

    3-3. In the Select Table dialog box, choose **Sheet1$**.
    (There are three worksheets in a document as a default. You used the
    first one. Sheets 2 and 3 in your file have no data.)

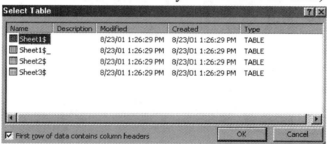

    3-4. Click **OK**.

4. From the Mail Merge Toolbar, choose **Mail Merge Recipients**.
   Mail Merge Recipients dialog box appears.

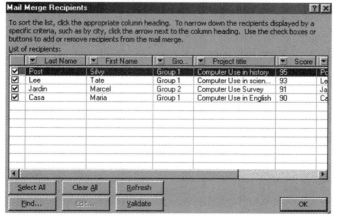

5. Let's filter the records and select only Group 1.
    5-1. From the Mail Merge Recipients dialog box, filter the data as you did in Activity 1 to show only Group 1.

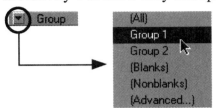

The database should be filtered as in the following figure.

	Last Name	First Name	Group	Project title	Score	
☑	Casa	Maria	Group 1	Computer Use in English	90	Casa
☑	Lee	Tate	Group 1	Computer Use in scien...	93	Lee
☑	Post	Silvy	Group 1	Computer Use in history	95	Post

    5-2. Click **OK**.

6. Let's merge the fields in the letter.
    6-1. To insert **«Salute»** field, click where the field should be placed in the word processing document.
    6-2. From the **Mail Merge Toolbar,** choose **Insert Merge Fields**.

    6-3. From the **Insert Merge Field** dialog box, click **Salute**.

    6-4. Click **Insert**.
    The field will be inserted in the letter.

```
Dear «Salute»
```

Be careful with spacing. There should be a space between **Dear** and **«Salute»**.

    6-5. Click **Close**.
    6-6. Merge the **Parent Name** field in the appropriate place of the letter. Don't forget the correct spacing!

6-7. Merge the **First Name** field in the appropriate place of the letter.

6-8. Merge the **Project Title** field in the appropriate place of the letter. You have just finished inserting fields into the letter.

7. Save the file LETTER.

8. Let's generate a new document and save the merged letters. You filtered the records to select Group 1 only. There were three records for Group 1. Therefore, three letters will be generated within one file.

8-1. From the **Mail Merge Toolbar**, choose **Merge to New Document**.

8-2. Choose **All** records as follows:

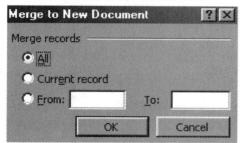

8-3. Click **OK**.
The letters will be generated.

8-4. Browse the letter.

8-5. Save the letters as MERGEDLETTER.

Project 2

In this project you will create labels by applying the data merge method. Creating labels is the same as creating form letters. When you finish, the labels will be similar to the following figure:

Silvy Post Group 1 Computer Use in history	Tate Lee Group 1 Computer Use in science	Marcel Jardin Group 2 Computer Use Survey
Maria Casa Group 1 Computer Use in English		

Use DATABASE1 as the data source. See the following instruction for Macintosh or Windows.

1. Create a new Word™ document.

2. Show the Data Merge Manager. (Tools menu → Data Merge Manager)

3. From the **Data Merge Manager** dialog box, choose **Main Document →
Create → Labels. . . .**

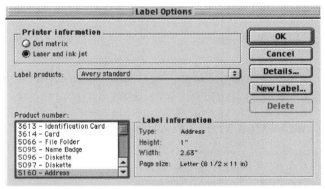

4. Choose the label.

The label code is Avery™ label codes. If you use a different brand, you
can find the corresponding Avery™ code from the label paper box. If you
don't have a label to print, don't worry. Just create the labels. We will
save it.

4-1. For this project, choose **5160—Address** as in the preceding figure.

4-2. Click **OK**.

The label outline will be inserted in the whole page.

	«Next Record»	«Next Record»
«Next Record»	«Next Record»	«Next Record»

5. Get the data source—DATABASE1.

(From Data Merge Manager, choose Data Source → Get Data → Open
Data Source. . . → find DATABASE1.) Select proper information in the
Open Worksheet dialog box.

The Edit Labels dialog box appears.

6. Merge Fields.
   6-1. From the Edit Labels dialog box, click **Insert Merge Field** button, and then choose the field to insert. Insert the fields as follows.

   «First_Name» «Last_Name»
   «Group»
   «Project_Title»

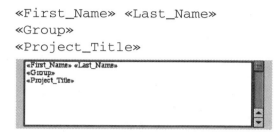

   6-2. Click **OK**.
        The fields will be shown in the labels.

«First_Name» «Last_Name» «Group» «Project_Title»	«Next Record»«First_Name» «Last_Name» «Group» «Project_Title»	«Next Record»«First_Name» «Last_Name» «Group» «Project_Title»
«Next Record»«First_Name» «Last_Name» «Group» «Project_Title»	«Next Record»«First_Name» «Last_Name» «Group» «Project_Title»	«Next Record»«First_Name» «Last_Name» «Group» «Project_Title»

7. Generate a new document and save the labels.
   7-1. Create a new document for the labels.
        (Merge → Merge to New Document).
   7-2. Save the labels as **DB2**.

1. Create a new Word™ document.

2. Show Mail Merge Toolbar.
   (**Tools** menu → **Letters and Mailings** → **Show Mail Merge Toolbar**)

3. Choose **Labels** as the Main Document Type.
   The Labels Dialog box appears:

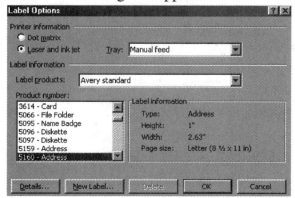

4. Choose the label.
   The label code is Avery™ label codes. If you use a different brand, you can find the corresponding Avery™ code from the label paper box. If you don't have a label to print, don't worry. Just create the labels. We will save it.

4-1. For this project, choose **5160—Address** as in the preceding figure.

4-2. Click **OK**.

The label outline will be inserted in the whole page.

5. Get the data source—DATABASE1.

The labels will be shown as follows:

	«Next Record»	«Next Record»
«Next Record»	«Next Record»	«Next Record»

6. Merge fields.

(Use the Mail Merge Toolbar → Insert Merge Fields.)

The labels will have a new look.

«First_Name» «Last_Name» «Group» «Project_title»	«Next Record»	«Next Record»
«Next Record»	«Next Record»	«Next Record»

7. Click **Propagate Labels** button from the Mail Merge Toolbar.

All the labels have fields inserted:

«First_Name» «Last_Name» «Group» «Project_title»	«Next Record»«First_Name» «Last_Name» «Group» «Project_title»	«Next Record»«First_Name» «Last_Name» «Group» «Project_title»
«Next Record»«First_Name» «Last_Name» «Group» «Project_title»	«Next Record»«First_Name» «Last_Name» «Group» «Project_title»	«Next Record»«First_Name» «Last_Name» «Group» «Project_title»

8. Generate a new document and save the labels.

8-1. Create a new document for the labels.

(Merge Toolbar → Merge to New Document).

8-2. Save the labels as **DB2**.

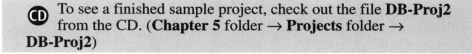

To see a finished sample project, check out the file **DB-Proj2** from the CD. (**Chapter 5** folder → **Projects** folder → **DB-Proj2**)

Integration with Other Programs

The most unique integration of database with other application programs is creating data merge (also called "mail merge") to create personalized letters (form letters) and labels. This feature makes teachers' work much easier when they send out letters to the parents. The basic information is the same and the students' names, parents' names, addresses, and other information can be personalized. This feature can be also applied to other tasks such as organizing students' projects to generate a report.

When a database program is used (not a spreadsheet as a database), the appearance of a database can be changed by adding graphics. Also, graphics or photos can be stored in the field.

Applications

In this chapter, the database hands-on skills for using Excel™ and the ideas for using database in the classroom were discussed. Examine the possibilities of applying database in education.

1. Collect ideas on how to use database with the students. You can refer to the section *Getting Started* to create your own ideas.

2. Collect ideas on how to use database as a teacher for classroom management and teaching. You can refer to the section *Getting Started* to create your own ideas. Consider the following example to get started:

Example

Activity Purpose: To organize the information necessary for the field trips.

Activity Description: Teachers can organize the information necessary for the field trips. The collected information could be date, location, address, contact person, phone number, guide name, cost. Also, the curriculum area (e.g., social studies, science, math, music, etc.) and the standards applied (State standards or any other standards, such as NCATE). Also, if possible, the related classroom activity can be recorded (this would be easier with a database program rather than a spreadsheet as a database).

The following database file was created with Excel™.

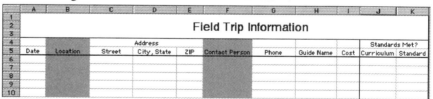

CD To examine the file, check out the file **FieldTrip** from the CD. (**Chapter 6** folder → **Applications** folder → **FieldTrip**)

When a similar database is created with a database program, it would look similar to the following figure:

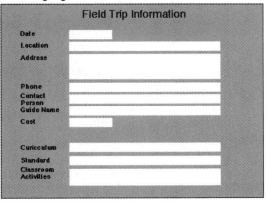

---

3. Create a lesson plan in which you can integrate database by expanding the ideas in the section *Getting Started* or by developing your own ideas. Include the following components:
   - Subject matter
   - Grade level
   - Purpose of the activity (lesson objective)
   - Target audience
     - Prior knowledge on the lesson objective (any related content covered?)
     - Computer skill
     - Any other information that you want to include
   - Environment
     - Location: In the classroom or in the lab?
     - Number of computers needed
   - Description of instructional activity
     - Description on how the lesson will proceed and how spreadsheet will be used

4. Collect ideas on how to integrate database with other programs. You can refer to the section *Integration with Other Programs* to create your own ideas.

Summary

1. Database is a computer program for organizing information. In this chapter, Excel™ was used for database.

2. There are various applications of the database program in education for students and teachers.

3. From the hands-on activities, the following tasks were covered:
   • Filtering data with AutoFilter and Custom Filter
   • Filling in the form
   • Sorting data
   • Merging data: Creating form letters and labels

Glossary

3-D Style The graphic tool used to transform a two-dimensional object into a three-dimensional (3-D) object.

Absolute Reference The unchanging value of the function when the function is copied and pasted (or Fill Right or Fill Down) into the next cell. *See* Relative Reference.

Active cell The current cell where the cursor is located in spreadsheet.

Animation In the PowerPoint™ presentation, this function gives special effects to a slide element, such as how to appear or disappear.

Argument The type of Lookup function calculation method in spreadsheet.

Array The compare range and the result range for the Lookup function in spreadsheet.

AutoFill Fills in the repetitive data automatically. The types of data are days of the week, months of the year, or sequential data.

AutoFilter In Excel™-based database, this function sets up the criteria within each field to filter the records.

AutoShapes A collection of objects that are commonly used shapes.

AutoSum A method to enter spreadsheet formula to calculate total(sum).

Background In the PowerPoint™ presentation, this function applies the fill-in background color to the slide master.

Bookmark Indicates a specific location to link the information in the web.

Borders The lines around the cells in spreadsheet and in a table. *See also* Shading.

Brightness Controls how dark or light the picture is.

Cell The intersection of a row and a column in spreadsheet or in a table.

Clip art A graphic that is ready to be used.

Collapsing the window Making the document window disappear visually while it is still open, particularly on Macintosh. *See* Minimizing the window.

Color Control Changes the color attributes of the picture: Automatic (Original), Grayscale, Black & White, and Watermark/Washout.

Column A vertical orientation of cells in spreadsheet or in a table.

Comment In spreadsheet, a comment can be added to the cell in order to keep a note. It does not affect the spreadsheet function such as calculation or sorting.

Compare range The criteria range that is set up for the Lookup function in spreadsheet.

Contrast Controls how sharply distinctive the elements in the picture are.

Cropping a Picture Selects part of the picture and keeps it.

Cross-platform The computer programs that are compatible between the platforms—Windows and Macintosh computers.

Custom animation As an advanced feature of animation in the PowerPoint™ presentation, this function deals with all the elements of the slide.

Custom Filter The mechanism to filter the records within the AutoFilter with the user-defined criteria in Excel.

Cut and Paste Moving text by using the commands from the menu. *See* Drag and Drop.

Data merge Creating customized letters, labels, or envelopes in a word processing file by inserting information from a database file.

Database Application software for organizing the information in fields and records.

Decimal precision The digits below the decimal point when the number format is chosen as Fixed in spreadsheet.

Dock As a new feature in MacOS X, it is a launching path to open programs, files, and other items that are used often.

Drag and Drop A method of moving text or an object within the document or copying to another document, by dragging it with the mouse and dropping it.

Drawing An object-oriented graphic program that is good for precise illustrations.

Effects In the PowerPoint™ presentation, this function controls how each element enters the slide and exits the slide as part of the custom animation.

Entry bar The location to enter data in spreadsheet.

Extension Three-digit letter to indicate the file type.

Field Place to hold specific information in database.

File (in database) A collection of records.

Fill Color Controls filling in color, pattern, and shadow.

Fill Down Spreadsheet feature for entering the same data in the vertical direction (in the column).

Fill Right Spreadsheet feature for entering the same data in the horizontal direction (in the row).

Filling color and effects Fills color, gradient, texture, pattern, and even a picture as the background of the picture.

Filtering data Selecting records by criteria and hiding the records that do not meet the criteria in database.

Followed hyperlink The hyperlink that was visited.

Footer An element of the page that appears in the bottom of the page. *See* Header.

Form A typical database format that was converted from the spreadsheet file.

Formula *See* Function.

Function A data type in spreadsheet that calculates numeric values according to a given formula.

Grouping Combining several objects to make one object in Drawing.

Hanging indent Indenting the whole paragraph, except the first line.

Header An element of the page that appears on top of the page. Various information can be included such as text, graphic, automatic page number, and current date and time. *See* Footer.

Hyperlink Links the element to the specified location.

Indentation In the PowerPoint™ presentation, this function promotes or demotes the text.

Indentation Leaving spaces in the beginning of a line or a paragraph in word processing.

Indentation markers Elements in the Ruler to control the paragraph indentations.

Inserting page number To have the computer calculate the page number of the document and place the page number in each page.

Keyboarding Using the fingers properly for typing.

Label Text data in spreadsheet.

Lassos Selection tool to select part of the picture.

Legend The list of explained items of the chart in spreadsheet.

Line Color Controls colors and patterns of a line.

Line spacing The space between the lines.

Line Style Controls the line weight (thickness).

Line Tool Graphic tool to draw lines.

Line weight Thickness of a line.

Lines Tool More line tools are available besides the simple straight line.

Linking In the PowerPoint™ presentation, this function activates a slide element to go to a particular slide.

List mode A mode in database to change the appearance of database to the list format.

Lookup The function in spreadsheet that assigns the value automatically based on the preset ranges—compare range and result range.

Lookup value The value that needs to be compared in Lookup function in spreadsheet.

Mail merge *See* Data merge.

Margin The empty space between the edge of the paper and the information on the paper.

Marquees Selection tool to select part of the picture.

Merging cells Combining two or more cells into one in spreadsheet and in a table.

Minimizing the window Making the document window disappear visually while it is still open. "Minimizing the window" is typically for Windows users. *See* Collapsing the window.

Notes The place in the PowerPoint™ presentation that holds the presenter's own reference information of the slide.

Object A unit—a shape—drawn in Drawing.

Office Assistant The animated character in MS Office that gives feedback for the questions that you typed in the box, or makes suggestions while you are working.

Order and timing In the PowerPoint™ presentation, this function controls (a) the sequence of the elements' entrance to the slide and exit from the slide, and (b) the method of such events—by mouse clicking or automatic timing.

Page break Mechanism that divides pages manually.

Page orientation The direction of the page, either vertical (also referred to as *portrait*) or horizontal (*landscape*). The default is the vertical orientation.

Painting A pixel-based bitmap graphic program that is good for digital paintings, photorealistic images, and freehand artistic graphics.

Paragraph spacing In the PowerPoint™ presentation, this function increases or decreases the spacing between lines.

Picture Effects Adds special effects to the picture.

Pixel Small dots that are the units for making a shape in Painting.

Platforms Types of personal computers—Windows and Macintosh computers.

Point Measurement unit for the font size.

Presentation A computer program that is designed to develop computer-based presentation material, especially for a large group.

Project Gallery The starting point in MS Office 2001 and v.X (Macintosh).

Record A collection of the fields in database.

Rectangle Tool Graphic tool used to draw rectangles or squares.

Recycle bin To delete the files and folders on Windows. *See* Trash.

Relative Reference The changing—relevant—value of the function when the function is copied and pasted (or Fill Right or Fill Down) into the next cell. *See* Absolute Reference.

Result range The interpretation range that is set up for the Lookup function in spreadsheet.

Row A horizontal orientation of cells in spreadsheet or in a table.

Save As One of the commands to save a document. When saving a document the first time, it is the same as Save. After that, Save As allows you to save the document as a different name or at a different location.

Select Objects Tool To select an object (a shape) that was drawn with drawing tools.

Shading Filling in color in the cell in spreadsheet and in a table. *See also* Borders.

Shadow Style The graphic tool used to add a shadow effect to a closed shape.

Shortcut Using the combination of the keys on the keyboard to perform some of the menu functions.

Slide A defined space in the presentation.

Slide Master Used in the PowerPoint™ presentation, it contains common elements for every slide such as text style for the title, text style for the main text, graphics, and buttons.

Slide show Viewing a computer-based presentation.

Slide transition A visual and/or sound effect added when advancing from one slide to another.

Sort Rearranging the data in ascending or descending order according to alphabetical or numerical criteria.

Spreadsheet Application software to manipulate numerical data.

Table Blocks of cells to enter and arrange text or graphic.

Task Pane A new feature in MS Office XP (Windows). It is shown in the right side of the screen and allows a quick access to the functions that are available in the menu.

Text alignment How to line up the text—to the left, to the right, to both sides, or to the center.

Text appearance Font, size, style, and color of the text.

Text Box Tool To type text in Drawing as if using a word processing program.

Text insertion point A form of cursor that is indicating the location to enter data.

Trash To delete the files and folders on Macintosh. Also used to eject disks and CDs. *See* Recycle bin.

Ungrouping Unlocking the grouped object to make individual objects in Drawing.

Value Number data in spreadsheet.

Word processing Application software for typing and editing text.

WordArt Preformatted and designed text in MS Office.

Wrapping text Arranging the text in relationship to a graphic.

Index

3-D object   94-95

Absolute Reference   168–172
Accessing programs in Microsoft Office   8–9
Active cell in spreadsheet   134
Alignment   52, 154–155
Animation   209–211
Application menu   25
Arrow Style   90
Arrowheads   90–91
AutoAverage   163–164
AutoCorrect   4
AutoFill   135–136
AutoFilter   245–246
AutoFormat   40–41
AutoMax   165
AutoMin   167
AutoShapes   92
AutoSum   136, 139

Bookmarks   119–120
Borders
    in spreadsheet cells   174–175
    in table   73–74
Brightness   106
Buttons   227–228

CD-R   7
CD-RW   7
Cell in spreadsheet   134
Chart in spreadsheet   140–143, 146
Checking the saved document   20
Clip art   60–62, 207
Close Box   26
Close Window   27
Closing a document window   26–28
Collapsing the document window   *See also*
          Minimizing the document window
Color
    Filling in graphic   105–106
    Text   54
Column
    Changing width   151–152
    Definition   134

Deleting   159–160
Inserting   159–160
Selecting   149
Comment in spreadsheet cell   155
Compare Range   169–172
Contrast   106
Creating
    a blank PowerPoint document   195–196
    a chart in spreadsheet   140–143
    a new document   9–10
    a new document within the program   24
    a page layout   110–117
    a PowerPoint document with a template
          185–187
    a spreadsheet document   133–134
    a web page   118–123
    a word processing document   37–38
    Form Letters   249–255
    Labels   255–258
Crop Tool   107–108
Cross-platform   2
Currency, number format in spreadsheet   153–154
Curve   90–91
Custom Animation   211–218
Custom Filter   246–247

Data Merge
    Creating Form Letters   249–255
    Creating Labels   255–258
    Definition   249
Database
    Data Merge   249–258
    Definition   238
    Features   238–239
    Filtering data   245–247   *See also* Filtering data
    Form   243–244
    in Microsoft Office   239–240
    in teaching and learning   240–241
    Setting up a database   242
    Showing All Records   247
    Sorting data   245
    Structure of database   243
    See also Spreadsheet
Date, number format in spreadsheet   159

Decimal Precision, number format in spreadsheet
     167–168
Deleting
     Column   159–160
     File   28–29
     Object   86
     Row   169
     Slide   204
     Text   48
Disk, out of the computer   21
Dock   8
Document
     Checking the saved document   20
     Closing a document window   26–28
     Collapsing the document window   11–13
     Minimizing the document window   11–13
     Printing a document   44
     Restoring the collapsed document   13
     Restoring the minimized document   13
     Saving a document with a different name   63
     Saving a new document   15–19
     Viewing the document in different size   43
     Working on multiple document   24–25
Drawing tools   84–85
Drawing   81   *See also* Graphic

Effects   213, 215
Effects, Filling in graphic   105–106
Entry Bar, in spreadsheet   134
Exiting the program   19
Extension   15

File
     Deleting a file   28–29
     Opening a file   23
Fill Down   148–149
Fill Right   147–148
Filtering data
     AutoFilter   245–246
     Custom Filter   246–247
First page, Different   59–60
Floppy disks   7
Followed hyperlink   226–227
Font   53
Footer
     in spreadsheet   143–144
     in word processing   42–43, 58–59
Form   243–244
Formatting Palette   4
Formula
     Mathematical formula   136
     See also Function
Freeform   90–91

Function
     AutoAverage   163–164
     AutoMax   165
     AutoMin   167
     AutoSum   136, 139
     Average   161–166
     Minimum   166–167
     Sum (Total)   136–139
     See also Formula

Graphic
     3-D object   94–95
     AutoShapes   92
     Brightness   106
     Color control   105
     Color, Filling   105–106
     Contrast   106
     Crop Tool   107–108
     Drawing   81
     Effects, Filling   105–106
     Graphic sources in Microsoft Office   82, 103
     in teaching and learning   82–83
     Lassos   108–109
     Lines Tool   90–91
     Marquees   108–109
     Page layout   110–117
     Painting   81
     Picture Effects   107
     Pixel   81
     Rectangle   88
     Shadowed object   95
     Square   88
     Text, Adding and editing   92–93
     WordArt   93–94
     Wrapping text   114–117
     See also Lines
     See also Object
Grouping objects   100–101

Hanging indent   68–69
Header
     in spreadsheet   143–144
     in word processing   42–43, 58–59
Highlight, text   54
Hyperlinking   *See* Linking
Hyperlinks   120–123

Indentation
     Definition   65–65
     Hanging indent   68–69
     in PowerPoint   205–206
     Indentation markers   66–69
     Indenting the first line with Tab key   66
     Indenting the whole paragraphs   67–68

Keyboard
    Command   14
    Control   14
    Differences in Windows and Macintosh   10–11

Landscape   38–39
Lassos   108–109
Legend   142
Line spacing   56
Lines
    Drawing lines   85–86
    Line weight, colors, and patterns   87–88
    with different appearances   87–88
Lines Tool
    Arrow Style   90
    Arrowheads   90–91
    Curve   90–91
    Freeform   90–91
    Scribble   90–91
Linking   225–229
Lookup   169–172

MacOS 9   2
MacOS X   2
Margins   62–63
Marquees   108–109
Merging cells
    in spreadsheet cells   172–173
    in table   72
Microsoft Office
    Accessing programs   8–9
    Different versions   2
    Graphic sources in Microsoft Office   82, 103
    Microsoft Office and different platforms   2–3
    New features in XP, 2001 and v.X   3
Minimizing the document window   11–13
Minimum   166–167
Motion Paths   4, 217–218
Movies   207–208
Multiple columns   112–113

Non-linear navigation in Presentation   182, 224–229
Notes   229–230
Number format in spreadsheet
    Currency   153–154
    Date   159
    Decimal Precision   167–168

Object
    3-D object   94–95
    Copying   87
    Definition   81
    Deleting   86

Filling in with color and effects   89
Flipping   96
Grouping   100–101
Moving   86
Moving to the back   98–99
Moving to the front   98–99
Pasting   87
Resizing   95
Rotating   96
Selecting   86
Selecting multiple objects   99–100
Shadowed object   95
Ungrouping   101
Office Assistant   25–26
Opening a file   23
Order and Timing   214, 216
Organization chart   221–223

Page break   56–58
Page number   58–59
Page orientation   38–39
Painting   81
Paragraph spacing in PowerPoint   205
Picture Effects   107
Pixel   81
Plain text   54
Platform   2
Point   53
Portrait   38–39
PowerPoint   *See* Presentation
Presentation
    Animation   209–211
    Buttons   227–228
    Creating a blank PowerPoint document   195–196
    Creating a PowerPoint document with a template   185–187
    Custom Animation   211–218
    Definition   182
    Effects   213, 215
    Features   182–183
    Followed hyperlink   226–227
    Graphics   207
    Hyperlinking   *See* Linking
    in teaching and learning   183
    Indentation   205–206
    Linking   225–229
    Motion Paths   217–218
    Movies   207–208
    Non-linear navigation   182, 224–229
    Notes   229–230
    Order and Timing   214, 216
    Organization chart   221–223
    Paragraph spacing   205

Printing   230–232
Saving as QuickTime Movie   232–233
Saving as Web Page   232
Slide   182, 187–188, 190–192, 196–200
   See also Slide
Sounds   208–209
Template   182, 185–187
Text   188–189
Text placeholders, Formatting   206–207
Viewing the presentation   192–193
Print Preview   44
Print Range in spreadsheet   145
Printing
in PowerPoint   230–232
in spreadsheet   144–145
in word processing   44
Project Gallery   3, 9

QuickTime movie   4, 232–233
Quitting the program   19

Rectangle   88
Recycle Bin   28–29
Relative Reference   168
Restoring the collapsed document   13
Restoring the minimized document   13
Result Range   169–172
Row
Changing height   152–153
Definition   134
Deleting   169
Inserting   169
Selecting   149
Row in table   73

Save As   63
Saving
a document as you work   50
a document with a different name   63
a new document   15–19
as QuickTime Movie in PowerPoint   232–233
as Web Page   123–124, 232
Checking the saved document   20
Scribble   90–91
Select Objects Tool   86
Shading
in spreadsheet cells   174–175
in table   73–74
Shortcuts   14
Showing All Records   247
Slide
Adding slide   190–192
Background   199–200
Browsing the slides   192

Definition   182
Deleting a slide   204
Rearranging the slides   204
Slide Layout   182, 187–188
Slide Master   196–199
Slide Transition   218–220
Sorting data   149–151, 245
Sounds   208–209
Spelling, Checking   41–42
Spreadsheet
Absolute Reference   168–172
Active cell   134
Alignment   154–155
AutoAverage   163–164
AutoFill   135–136
AutoMax   165
AutoMin   167
AutoSum   136, 139
Average   161–166
Borders   174–175
Cell   134
Chart   140–143, 146
Column   134, 149, 151–152, 159–160
Comment   155
Compare Range   169–172
Creating a spreadsheet document   133–134
Data types   140
Definition   130
Entering data manually   135
Entering data with AutoFill function 135–136
Entry Bar   134
Features   130–131
Fill Down   148–149
Fill Right   147–148
Footer   143–144
Header   143–144
in teaching and learning   131–132
Legend   142
Lookup   169–172
Mathematical formula   136
Maximum   164–166
Merging cells   172–173
Minimum   166–167
Number format   153–154, 159   *See also*
   Number format in spreadsheet
Decimal Precision   167–168
Print Range   145
Printing   144–145
Relative Reference   168
Result Range   169–172
Row   134, 149, 152–153, 161
Shading   174–175
Sorting data   149–151
Sum (Total)   136–139

Text style   151
See also Database
Square   88
Storage devices   6–7
Style, Text   53
Sum (Total)   136–139

Table   69–74
    Adding   69–70
    Borders   73–74
    Column size, Changing   70
    Columns, Distributing evenly   70
    Entering text in the table   71–72
    Formatting text in the table   72
    Merging cells   72
    Row, Changing the size   73
    Shading   73–74
Task Pane   3, 10
Template in PowerPoint   182, 185–187
Text
    Copying text   49–50
    Deleting text   48
    Entering text   39–41
    Entering text in the table   71–72
    Formatting text   51–63, 65–74
    Formatting text in the table   72
    in Drawing   92–93
    in Presentation (PowerPoint)   188–189
    in Spreadsheet   151
    Inserting text   46–47
    Moving text   48–49
    Pasting text   49–50
    Selecting text   47
    Text alignment   52
    Text appearance   52–55
    Text insertion point   39
Toolbars
    Definition   15
    Drawing tools   84–85
    in Presentation (PowerPoint)   190
    Picture formatting tools   104
    Viewing   51–52
Trash   28–29

Undoing   48
Ungrouping object   101

Viewing the document in different size   43

Web page
    Creating   118–123
    Previewing   123
    Saving as Web Page   123–124, 232
Word processing
    Alignment   52
    Checking spelling   41–42
    Clip art   60–62
    Copying text   49–50
    Creating a web page   118–123
    Creating a word processing document   37–38
    Definition   33
    Deleting text   48
    Entering text   39–41
    Features   33–34
    First page, Different   59–60
    Footer   42–43, 58–59
    Formatting text   51–63, 65–74
    Header   42–43, 58–59
    in teaching and learning   34–35
    Indentation   65–69
    Inserting text   46–47
    Line spacing   56
    Margins   62–63
    Moving text   48–49
    Multiple columns   112–113
    Page break   56–58
    Page layout   110–117
    Page number   58–59
    Page orientation   38–39
    Pasting text   49–50
    Print Preview   44
    Printing a document   44
    Saving as Web Page   123–124
    Selecting text   47
    Table   69–74 (*See* Table)
    Text appearance   52–55
    Undoing   48
    Viewing the document in different size   43
    Wrapping text   114–117
WordArt   93–94
Wrapping text   114–117

Zip disks   7